International Federation of Library Associations and Institutions
Fédération Internationale des Associations de Bibliothécaires et des Bibliothèques
Internationaler Verband der bibliothekarischen Vereine und Institutionen
Международная Федерация Библиотечных Ассоциаций и Учреждений
Federación Internacional de Asociaciones de Bibliotecarios y Bibliotecas
国际图书馆协会与机构联合会
الاتحاد الدولي لجمعيات ومؤسسات المكتبات

About IFLA www.ifla.org

IFLA (The International Federation of Library Associations and Institutions) is the leading international body representing the interests of library and information services and their users. It is the global voice of the library and information profession.

IFLA provides information specialists throughout the world with a forum for exchanging ideas and promoting international cooperation, research, and development in all fields of library activity and information service. IFLA is one of the means through which libraries, information centres, and information professionals worldwide can formulate their goals, exert their influence as a group, protect their interests, and find solutions to global problems.

IFLA's aims, objectives, and professional programme can only be fulfilled with the cooperation and active involvement of its members and affiliates. Currently, approximately 1,600 associations, institutions and individuals, from widely divergent cultural backgrounds, are working together to further the goals of the Federation and to promote librarianship on a global level. Through its formal membership, IFLA directly or indirectly represents some 500,000 library and information professionals worldwide.

IFLA pursues its aims through a variety of channels, including the publication of a major journal, as well as guidelines, reports and monographs on a wide range of topics. IFLA organizes workshops and seminars around the world to enhance professional practice and increase awareness of the growing importance of libraries in the digital age. All this is done in collaboration with a number of other non-governmental organizations, funding bodies and international agencies such as UNESCO and WIPO. IFLANET, the Federation's website, is a prime source of information about IFLA, its policies and activities: www.ifla.org

Library and information professionals gather annually at the IFLA World Library and Information Congress, held in August each year in cities around the world.

IFLA was founded in Edinburgh, Scotland, in 1927 at an international conference of national library directors. IFLA was registered in the Netherlands in 1971. The Koninklijke Bibliotheek (Royal Library), the national library of the Netherlands, in The Hague, generously provides the facilities for our headquarters. Regional offices are located in Rio de Janeiro, Brazil; Pretoria, South Africa; and Singapore.

IFLA Publications 154

Designing Library Space for Children

Edited by
Ingrid Bon, Andrew Cranfield
and Karen Latimer

De Gruyter Saur

IFLA Publications
edited by Sjoerd Koopman

ISBN 978-3-11-023216-5
e-ISBN 978-3-11-023217-2
ISSN 0344-6891

Library of Congress Cataloging-in-Publication Data

Designing library space for children / edited by Ingrid Bon, Andrew Cranfield, and Karen Latimer.
   p. cm. -- (IFLA publications, ISSN 0344-6891 ; 154)
   Papers presented at a joint session of the Library Buildings and Equipment and the Libraries for Children and Young Adults sections at the IFLA World Congress in Milan in 2009 under the title "If I was the Library Director."
   Includes bibliographical references.
   ISBN 978-3-11-023216-5 (alk. paper)
   1. Libraries--Space utilization--Congresses. 2. Library buildings--Design and construction--Congresses. 3. Library architecture--Congresses. 4. Children's libraries--Congresses. 5. Young adults' libraries--Congresses. I. Bon, Ingrid. II. Cranfield, Andrew. III. Latimer, Karen. IV. International Federation of Library Associations and Institutions. Section on Library Buildings and Equipment. V. International Federation of Library Associations and Institutions. Libraries for Children and Young Adults Section. VI. World Library and Information Congress (75th : 2009 : Milan, Italy)
   Z679.55.D47 2011
   022'.31625--dc23
                                                        2011041195

Bibliographic information published by the Deutsche Nationalbibliothek
The Deutsche Nationalbibliothek lists this publication in the Deutsche Nationalbibliografie; detailed bibliographic data is available in the Internet
at http://dnb.d-nb.de.

Walter de Gruyter GmbH & Co. KG, Berlin/Boston

∞ Printed on permanent paper
The paper used in this publication meets the minimum requirements of American National Standard – Permanence of Paper for Publications and Documents in Libraries and Archives ANSI/NISO Z39.48-1992 (R1997)

Cover image: The Red Thread in Hjoerring, Denmark

Typesetting: Dr. Rainer Ostermann, München
Printing and binding: Strauss GmbH, Mörlenbach

Printed in Germany

www.degruyter.com

Contents

Introduction

If I was the Library Director...

Recent years have seen renewed focus on and interest in library architecture, design language and how we think libraries should be spatially renewed. There seems to be a general consensus that if libraries and library services are to remain relevant in a digital era, then it will be necessary to re-evaluate and rethink how libraries should look in the 21st century. We have seen a number of interesting and imaginative new library buildings and refurbishments, both in academic and public libraries, but far too often it has, unfortunately, been business as usual. New, and undoubtedly impressive, architectural projects often rather seem to lack an understanding of how, and in what ways, information and knowledge are disseminated in modern society – and where the merging of traditional media with new electronic media lacks imagination and a real understanding of what patrons want and demand of future library services. The library community's rather conservative stance when it comes to the design of libraries is cause for concern – we still can learn a lot from the world of museums and, not least, from the retail trade and high street marketing.

Nowhere is this more evident than in the world of children's libraries and in the need to address the issue that this generation of children may come to use the library as an institution much less than the generation before them; and while libraries still play an important role for primary and secondary education, as well as supporting literacy and cultural diversity, there is little room for complacency. Many of us have seen and visited libraries for children which are more or less as we remember them from our own childhood, where the odd play station and a selection of DVDs are only a small part of the answer.

If we really want to improve facilities for children in our libraries we need a better understanding of a number of cross-disciplinary fields, not least media understanding and media usage by children and young adults as well as learning patterns and trends in modern education.

At the IFLA World Congress in Milan in 2009 two of IFLA's sections joined forces (Library Buildings and Equipment and Libraries for Children and Young Adults) to present a number of papers under the title of "If I was the Library Director…" which included two keynote contributions with a broad focus followed by a number of interesting and challenging examples of children's library design from around the world.

The first keynote paper from Alistair Black, University of Illinois, and Carolynn Rankin, Leeds Metropolitan University, gives us some historical background with a discussion of the history of children's library design. The libraries that we have for children today did not just appear out of the blue, but are, of course, very visible products of society's changing views of childhood and children and, as the authors write in their introduction, "buildings are a product of society's beliefs and aspirations". We think it is imperative that we understand and have knowledge of developments over the last century in order to make informed decisions about the future. Black and Rankin bring our attention to the whole question of regulation – i.e. regulation of behaviour which in this case relates to discipline where the library can be seen as a continuum of school discipline and also the fact that libraries for children were essentially conceptualised in the same way as schools. Over time this consensus and understanding changed as libraries became thought of as public spaces dislocated from what one might call the "controlled" space of the educational facility. The authors chart a change of perception about children and the rise of the Child Guidance movement of the 1920s and 1930s which sought to help children and heralded a new understanding of the child as both an individual and a citizen.

Black and Rankin go on to present a number of new and groundbreaking library designs for children giving the reader valuable insight into developments of the early and mid 20th century. As is so often the case history repeats itself – discussions of the 1950s show the ever present dichotomy of established and recognised cultural forms against the tide of popular culture artefacts – most readers will, to some extent, recognise these debates from the way we think of the design of children's libraries in the 21st century, and how we are still unsure of which road to travel down. While developments show a better understanding and acceptance of the idea of childhood, youth and young adults the authors show that "a great many children's libraries of the 1960s appear to take their cue from the office environment, providing workmanlike tables alongside more comfortable furniture", and one might argue that librarians and library designers are only now coming to grips with a new design paradigm for the children's library.

Moving into the 1980s the idea of community librarianship comes alive in Britain and other countries, where libraries take on a more socially proactive role in relation to the local community, and the role of the librarian can be seen to change from a passive disseminator of information to a much more proactive identity with an active involvement with the library patron. These trends are, to some extent, reflected in the more recent design of libraries – both in relation to adults and children – with influences from the retail business and the high street as visible testaments to changing perceptions and roles of libraries. Much has been both written and said about the Idea Stores in the London borough of Tower Hamlets, but there is little doubt that these new library buildings reflect both a new spirit of (local) community engagement and a more "youthful" design.

Kirsten Drotner, in her contribution to this publication entitled *Children's media culture: a key to libraries of the future* gives the reader valuable insight into how children and young adults use modern media and technology in their everyday lives. An understanding of how media usage is changing is undoubtedly highly important in our future endeavours when designing and constructing libraries for the children of today and of the future. In the past media usage could, to some extent, be divided into non-commercial (public service) and commercial (often financed by advertising) services, but the question we have to ask ourselves is whether this distinction is any longer of relevance or perhaps more importantly – possible to uphold. Media convergence – both technological, economic and cross border – makes it more and more impossible to differentiate between "good" media and "bad" media. Google, Facebook, Twitter and other social communication tools force libraries and librarians to think "out of the box" if libraries and their young users are to find common ground. Drotner emphasises the participatory nature of modern media, which changes the focus from physical collections and passive access to user involvement and innovation and what Drotner describes as *semiotic competence* – i.e. "the ability to give shape to and handle multimodal expressions as part of everyday collaboration, communication and participation".

Children's use of new media is both complex and multi-faceted, making the challenge for those that design libraries and those who work in them ever more pressing. Drotner emphasises the need for new professional skills and what she describes as "holistic strategies for communication with users", and we think it is safe to assume that a whole new way of communicating with library users, old as well as young, dictates new visions for how we design and organise our libraries.

The remaining contributions to this publication take us on a journey around the globe investigating practical ways in which librarians and architects have sought to rethink strategies for children's library design. It is our hope that these essays will provide inspiration and reflection as to how we might translate theory and lessons learnt from the past into more proactive and ambitious thinking when planning how our libraries should look in the future.

We would very much like to thank all our colleagues in the Standing Committees for both the IFLA Section for Library Buildings and Equipment and the IFLA Section for Libraries for Children and Young Adults and not least to Sjoerd Koopman at IFLA HQ who has supported this publication from the outset. Thanks also go to Simone van Rijn and Susan Feeney who transformed the text into publishable format.

Ingrid Bon
Chair, Section Libraries for Children and Young Adults 2007-2011

Karen Latimer
Chair, Section for Library Buildings and Equipment 2008-2011

Andrew Cranfield
Chair, Section for Library Buildings and Equipment 2004-2007

Conference Papers

The History of Children's Library Design: Continuities and Discontinuities

Alistair Black
University of Illinois, USA
and
Carolynn Rankin
Leeds Metropolitan University, UK

Like all technology, buildings are a product of society's beliefs and aspirations. Thus, the built form of the children's library, a distinct 'designed space', or 'building type', since the late-nineteenth century, can only be fully understood if studied in relation to accompanying social forms. Accordingly, this paper pays close attention to the various purposes that have underpinned children's library work over the past century – purposes articulated by librarians, library providers, reformers and commentators that were, in turn, rooted in broader social, economic, political and cultural developments. In setting the scene, it is also appropriate at various points in the discussion to say something about certain broad developments in architecture and design that might be seen to have impacted on the design of the children's library.

Our analysis is divided into four periods: before the First World War; the inter-war years; the post-Second World War decades to about 1980; and the post-1980 period. Each of these periods of children's library design is characterised by distinct themes, some of which were at the time new, some of which had manifested themselves in earlier phases; and these continuities and discontinuities are summarised in the paper's conclusion. Our geographical focus is primarily Britain, although mention is also made of developments in, and influences from, abroad, most notably the United States.

Our primary sources for this paper have been varied: the *Library Association Record* (UK), first published in 1899; archival material, including photographs, located in the collections of municipal local studies libraries; books and chapters in books contemporaneous with the events and periods we have studied; and, in relation to recent developments, evidence from our own visits to children's libraries and from websites documenting or promoting individual children's libraries.[1]

---

1   Including, for example, the 'Designing Libraries' website: http://www.designinglibraries.org. uk/ [viewed September 2011].

Before 1914: School and shelter

It was not until the end of the nineteenth century that library provision for children on anything approaching the scale or in the form we see today began. A number of factors coalesced to bring this about. In the closing decades of the nineteenth century, the development of the public library in Britain, which had commenced in 1850, finally began to accelerate swiftly, facilitating and legitimising the emergence of specialised services, including services for the young. The growth of specialisms was supported by the development of professional librarianship following the establishment of the Library Association in 1877. A number of librarians became keenly interested in the library needs of children and began to write extensively in the library press about the issue.[2] This is not to say, however, that there existed any specialist training for children-focus librarians, nor that specialist posts were created and advertised. Only three dedicated posts before the First World have been identified: at Nottingham (1897), Cardiff (1907) and Leicester (1910).[3] This contrasted markedly with children's provision in the United States which British librarians studied and admired.[4]

Increased demand for children's facilities came from the growth of children's literacy following the arrival of state education in 1870. On the 'supply side', children's publishing improved markedly. A rapid increase in the number and quality of books and magazines aimed at children occurred in the second half of the nineteenth century. Librarians hoped that 'good' reading would turn children away from 'the perniciousness of the penny horrible',[5] and the 'garbage' written for them in half-penny 'funnies' and 'comics' which had, as one library commentator believed, 'the most lamentable influence on their future character'.[6]

An early practical reason for the introduction of the children's library was to create more space, as well as quiet, for adult readers by removing the adolescent boys who populated libraries in relatively large numbers. Segregating

---

2   W.C.B. Sayers, *The children's library: a practical manual for public, school and home libraries* (London: Routledge, 1911), pp. 204-213 contains an extensive ten-page bibliography on children's libraries.

3   A. Ellis, *Library services for young people in England and Wales 1830-1970* (Oxford: Pergamon Press, 1971), pp. 34-35.

4   For example, see S. Fairchild, 'What American libraries are doing for children and young people', *Library Association Record*, Vol. 5 (1903), pp. 549-551, and L.S. Jast, 'Some impressions of American libraries', *Library Association Record*, Vol. 7 (1905), p. 67. Brief histories of children's libraries in America are given by M. Sassé, 'The children's librarian in America', *Library Journal* (15 January 1973), pp. 213-216, and E.L. Power, *Work with children in public libraries* (Chicago: American Library Association, 1943). Effie Power was a pioneer of children's libraries in the America in the early-twentieth century.

5   *Islington Gazette* (23 January 1908).

6   B. Carter, 'School libraries', *Library World*, Vol. 8 (1905), p. 29.

the juvenile from the adult was the desirable, though not the practical and economic, option for many librarians, and was certainly appealing to adult readers seeking order and quiet. Separate accommodation was given over to juvenile readers in the Manchester Public Library in 1861.[7] A separate building for children was first supplied in 1882, in Nottingham.[8] In Wigan in 1895, a building was opened to house a separate boy's library as well as a committee room.[9]

In the decades immediately approaching the First World War, children's sections in adult accommodation – a convenient device for serving children – gradually became less popular and unnecessary as dedicated children's rooms became more common. Separate accommodation often meant separate entrances for adults and children. At Hove Public Library, opened in 1908, the library was located in the basement, accessed by a separate entrance to the side of the building. The same arrangement was implemented at Bury, though the room there was at street level.[10] After 1918 separate entrances for children and adults girls were generally not seen in designs for new libraries, the plan for the extension to Scarborough Public Library (1936) being an exception.[11]

The children's library was often divided into separate accommodation for boys and girls. At Kingston District Library, Glasgow, the first Carnegie library to be opened in the City, boys and girls were kept apart by a glass screen, the superintendent's desk straddling the room's segregated compartments, thereby allowing direct supervision over both areas. In unisex rooms, it was advised that boys' and girls' periodicals be grouped on separate tables.[12] In late-nineteenth century Manchester a string of boys' rooms – ten by 1899 – were opened. The name was an anomaly as 'girls were admitted equally with boys'.[13] The rooms had a good amount of space devoted to them in the branches in which they were located – in places over half the amount of space enjoyed by adult readers.[14]

As the age at which children left school rose and children left the workforce (more about this later), designing environments for children to pursue the non-work activities of learning and playing became more important. Moreover, as industrialisation and urbanisation matured, and as concern for order and discipline grew, regulated and architecturally constructed public spaces for

7 Ellis, *Library services for young people in England and Wales*, op. cit., pp. 3-4.
8 T. Kelly, *A history of public libraries in Great Britain, 1845-1975* (London: Library Association, 1977), p. 53.
9 *Programme of the presentation to the Borough of the Boy's Reading Room, April 17th 1895* (Wigan, 1895).
10 A. Sparke, 'Bury juvenile library', *Library World*, Vol. 5 (1903), p. 233.
11 W.H. Smettem, 'Extensions to the Scarborough Public Library', *Library Association Record*, Vol. 39, (February 1937), p. 58.
12 Sayers, *The children's library*, op. cit., p. 82.
13 L.S. Jast, *The child as reader* (London: Libraco, 1927), p. 26.
14 W.R. Credland, *The Manchester public free libraries* (Manchester: Manchester Public Free Libraries, 1899), p. 283.

Figure 1. Juvenile Reading Rooms, Kingston District Library, Glasgow (opened 1904).
Source: *Descriptive Handbook of the Glasgow Corporation Public Libraries*
(Glasgow: Glasgow Corporation Libraries Committee, 1907).

children, including children's libraries, became much more common.[15] Regulation was certainly at the heart of early children's library design. Even allowing for the dangers of retrospective history, compared to today's children's libraries the look of the majority of spaces allocated to children before the First World War was stern, barren, uninspiring, mean and dull. The initial inclination of librarians was to conceptualise the physical arrangements in, and decoration of, children's spaces along the same lines as the treatment of adult spaces. For many, the children's library served as a mere *shelter*, a place of refuge from inhospitable streets and crowded, squalid homes. The early children's room also had the feel of the *schoolroom*. Rectangular tables organised in neat rows were designed, as in the schoolroom, to instil discipline and good behaviour. (Although it is important to emphasise that the early children's library was not always a place of discipline. Any strategy or mechanism of control can attract resistance. The children's library has been no exception in this regard. For those who viewed the children's room as a symbol of author-

---

15 M. Gutman and N. De Conick-Smith (eds.), *Designing modern childhoods: history, space and the material culture of children* (Rutgers University Press, 2008).

ity, it was a place in which to make trouble).[16] Tables or desks allowed the reader to face only one way, in the tradition of the school and the church: tables allowing readers to sit on one side only was ideal, said the librarian J.D. Stewart: 'this arrangement promotes good order', he argued, whereas round tables gave rooms 'a confused appearance'.[17] The importance of colour and an attractive décor were barely considered; in 1885, three years after it opened, the children's library in Nottingham was merely whitewashed.[18]

Despite the tendency towards decorative austerity, by the early-twentieth century librarians and library designers had begun to think in a much more focused way about the physical arrangements for children and young people. A pioneer in the field was Cardiff's librarian, John Ballinger, who preached that "children must be provided for by a separate and special effort". The children's room, he said, should take "exactly the same position of importance and size as the adults' room ... The children must not be pushed away". [19] Ballinger's children's rooms in Cardiff were described as "lofty, well-lighted and ventilated ... [and] decorated with pictures".[20] Enlightened librarians like Ballinger came to realise that children did not need 'libraries' so much as 'reading halls': rooms with a relaxed, non-school atmosphere where the young could undertake non-book activities, be directed in their reading and look at the illustrated papers. Ballinger conceptualised the 'reading hall' – as opposed to the 'library' or the associated term 'reading room' – as a softer description of the space for children (but he objected to the idea of Peterborough's librarian, W.J. Willcock, of calling them simply 'recreation rooms').[21] 'Halls' were to be places to which children could bring their own books, where they could engage in non-book activities and feel happy about staying for long periods: they should not simply be places for lending books for home reading.

In British library circles the idea took root that services to children should take a cue from the nurturing, sympathetic environments created in American children's libraries. Croydon Public Library's Stanley Jast was highly enthusiastic about the children's libraries he saw on a visit to the United States in 1903:

---

16 As symbols of authority, libraries certainly experienced their fair share of disaffection on the part of children and young people. When a reading room was opened at a Board School in Leyton in 1898, the Chairman of the Library Committee trusted that 'those who used the room would help the Assistant to keep order, and that they would be troubled by no unruly boys': *Leyton Public Library Quarterly Library Magazine*, Vol. 1 (1898).

17 J.D. Stewart et al., *Open access libraries: their planning, equipment and organisation* (London: Grafton, 1915), p. 88.

18 Nottingham Public Libraries Sub-Committee Minutes (27 May 1885).

19 J. Ballinger, 'Children's reading halls', *Library Association Record*, Vol. 5 (1903), p. 553.

20 W.C.B. Sayers, *A manual of children's libraries* (London: Allen and Unwin, 1932), p. 104.

21 Ballinger, 'Children's reading halls', op. cit., pp. 552-558. See, also, W.J. Willcock,. 'Are children's libraries really necessary?', [Letter to] *Library Association Record*, Vol. 7 (1907), pp. 184-185, and the response by J. Ballinger, in the same volume, pp. 354-355.

The children's rooms which you get in all the new buildings are exceedingly fine, beautiful apartments, the woodwork often beautifully carved, and so on. At the recently opened Pacific Branch at Brooklyn there is a magnificent fireplace and an ingle-nook in which the children can sit close to the fire on winter evenings and read their books ... There are good pictures on the walls, and the higher shelves are covered with wooden flaps, [in turn] covered with green baize, on which pictures are fastened. The whole appearance of the room is bright and gay, the appeal being constantly to the eye as well as the mind of the child.[22]

Berwick Sayers, a leading advocate of children's libraries, was impressed by the nature-oriented pursuits provided in some American libraries: on 'flower days' children might be invited to bring blooming wild flowers to the library, which were used to decorate the room and provide raw material for study with the aid of books on botany.[23] The old theory, said Sayers, was that "given space, a stool to sit upon and something to read, the child was satisfied", but what he, Sayers, wanted was rooms "which will give to the child generally most of the characteristics of a private study".[24] Because "the child comes naturally in search of beautiful and pleasant things" in the realms of knowledge, Sayers calculated, the surroundings also needed to be pleasant and beautiful.[25]

The children's room Sayers created at Wallasey Public Library before the First World War was, he recalled, "a homely room with a large bay window giving onto the lawn, around the interior of which I ran a continuous window seat".[26] 'The ideal children's department', said Sayers, is a well lighted, lofty apartment, well-furnished and decorated, and properly staffed – an attractive or even beautiful apartment, equal in status to any other department of the municipal library. While its immediate object is utilitarian, it should have in addition an aesthetic ideal; and the rather prevalent conceptions that a room in the basement in charge of a janitor or boy assistant will suffice, or that children are admitted only on sufferance to a library that is really for adults, should perish.[27]

Sayers' complete formula for a popular and busy children's library comprised an attractive reading room with books on open access, located around the walls, the space flexible enough to be transformed into a lecture room with 'performance' platform at one end. Separate rooms for a reference collection and storytelling completed the accommodation.

However, the liberal and progressive ideas of librarians like Ballinger and Sayers were the exception rather than the rule and were not widely translated

---

22   L.S. Jast, 'Some impressions of American libraries', *Library Association Record*, Vol. 7 (1905), pp. 63-64.

23   Sayers, *The children's library*, op. cit., p. 88.

24   Sayers, *A manual of children's libraries*, op. cit., p. 112.

25   Sayers, *The children's library*, op. cit., p. 90.

26   W.C.B. Sayers, 'Children's libraries as I saw them', *Library World*, Vol. 60 (1958), p. 23.

27   Sayers, *The children's library*, op. cit., p. 79.

into the physical environment of the children's library. In the pre-1914 period the largely design-free shelter mentality dominated. This was linked to prevailing anxiety concerning the degeneration of the British race. It was believed that libraries could help elevate the young by rescuing them from the morally and physically damaging recreational life of the street, made all the more sinister by an awareness of the puzzling persistence of poverty.[28] Fear of the consequences of the street and the promises that libraries gave to ameliorate these fears were fuelled, of course, by anxieties, compounded by stiffening foreign competition, concerning the bodily and mental decline of the population: a degeneration of the race, comprising a deterioration in national intelligence and in the physical condition of the masses. The "future of the race... depends upon the enrichment of the imaginative life of the race", wrote Stanley Jast.[29] One of the purposes of early children's libraries was clearly that of 'child rescue' – the protection of children from social and biological degradation.

In various ways, therefore, children's libraries became part of the pre-First World War 'national efficiency' movement. This explains why many of the early spaces – if they went beyond the need merely to offer shelter – adopted the form of the schoolroom. Fears of economic decline relative to advancing nations like Germany and the United States coalesced with nagging doubts about the moral fabric of mass society. This resulted in louder calls for improved education, including technical instruction and library provision. It is no coincidence that the design of, and spatial arrangements in, some early children's rooms mirrored that of the traditional school and schoolroom, including the segregation of boys and girls, reflective of the distinctive roles allotted to the sexes in the quest for industrial and imperial survival: women as homemakers, providing a nurturing environment for the nation's future male workers and soldiers.[30]

The 1920s and 1930s: Middle-class domesticity and constructive play

What one might describe as the 'coming of age' of the children's library between the wars coincided with the growth of initiatives and ideas, which had begun to emerge in the late-Victorian and Edwardian years, concerning childhood and child welfare. These ideas heralded what Hendrick believes can reasonably be termed 'modern childhood', in that during this period childhood

28   On the persistence of poverty, see G.S. Jones, *Outcast London: a study in the relationship between classes in Victorian society* (Oxford: Clarendon Press, 1971).

29   Jast, *The child as reader*, op. cit., p. 40.

30   A. Davin, 'Imperialism and motherhood', *History Workshop Journal*, Vol. 5, No. 1 (1978), pp. 9-66.

was 'legally, legislatively, socially, medically, psychologically, educationally and politically institutionalised'.[31] There arose 'a belief, incomprehensible to earlier generations, that children are citizens who have social rights independent of their parents, rights which the state has a duty to protect'.[32] The lot of children had been improved by a number of legislative initiatives, including the raising of the compulsory school-leaving age to 14 in 1918 and of the age of sexual consent to 16 in 1885, and the introduction of school meals and school medical inspection in 1906 and 1907, respectively. The Children's Act (1908) established juvenile courts and a system of registration of foster parents. Consequently, it could be said that by the inter-war period children had become, in a sense, 'children of the state'.[33]

As British imperial and industrial pre-eminence became threatened by high infant mortality and low levels of working-class health,[34] there was growing discussion about the physical and mental condition of the nation and the political and social consequences of poverty. The establishment of a child study movement in the United States (a Child Study Association was founded in 1894, growing out of the psychological teachings of the American child psychologist G. Stanley Hall) impacted considerably on the thinking and policies of child welfare specialists in Britain. The Child Guidance movement of the 1920s and 1930s attempted to treat and cure, through psychiatric clinics, nervous, maladjusted and delinquent children. These and other developments in child psychology and psychiatry reflected a new understanding of childhood, a realisation that childhood mattered.[35] The twentieth century had become 'century of the child'.[36]

In the field of education a number of progressive ideas took root. In the United States, Hall had differentiated between the 'scholiocentric' and the

---

31   H. Hendrick, *Children, childhood and English society 1880-1990* (Cambridge: Cambridge University Press), p. 15. The study of the history of childhood was effectively inaugurated by Philippe Ariès's *Centuries of Childhood* (London: Cape, 1962). His statement that the concept of childhood did not exist until the seventeenth century eventually attracted strong criticism, but it at least served to place the issue of the social significance of children on the historical map, and to rescue children from history in the same way that women's history has written women back into the historical record.

32   I. Pinchbeck and M. Hewitt, *Children in English society. Volume II: from the eighteenth century to the Children's Act 1948* (London: Routledge and Kegan Paul, 1973), p. 637.

33   'Children of the state' is the title to Chapter XXI, pp. 638-656, of Pinchbeck and Hewitt, op. cit.

34   A. Davin, *Growing up poor: home, school and street in London 1870-1914* (London: Rivers Oram Press, 1996), p. 153.

35   H. Hendrick, 'Constructions and reconstructions of British childhood: an interpretive survey, 1800 to the present', in A. James and A. Prout (eds.), *Constructing and reconstructing childhood* (London: Routledge Farmer, 1997), pp. 47-49, 51-53.

36   J. Clarke, 'Histories of childhood', in D. Wyse, *Childhood studies: an introduction* (Oxford: Blackwell, 2004), pp. 10-11.

'pedocentric' school. In the former the needs of the institution came first; in the latter, the needs of the child were prioritised and the stages of child development determined the content and format of teaching.[37] Hall taught that the guardians of the young should defend "the happiness of the rights of children" and should understand that "there is nothing else so worthy of love, reverence, and service as the body and soul of the growing child".[38] Progressive education theory placed the child at the centre of the education process. It was advocated that schools should provide an environment in which individuals could be shareholders in determining and achieving common learning goals. All pupils would undertake experiential education – learning by doing – which tapped into their natural curiosity and energy. Education was to be a process in which the child learned how to solve problems and did not simply learn by rote. Education through play and self-expression, through dance for example, was encouraged.[39] The Montessori method, developed by Maria Montessori in the opening decade of the twentieth century, emphasised spontaneous activity, freedom of choice of activities and self-development through movement. This pedagogy was deeply dependent on a sensitively 'prepared environment': surroundings needed to be attractive and well-decorated, with furniture and fittings appropriate to the ages and needs of children.[40] Such thinking was in the tradition of the Froebelian method developed in the nineteenth century, for which Sayers showed great sympathy.

The expanding interest in child psychology and welfare appeared to infiltrate the thinking of some librarians. The notion that by the early-twentieth century children had begun to 'matter', is illustrated in the growing number of writings on children's libraries. An early major contribution was Sayers' *The children's library* (1911).[41] Sayers observed that: "More recently it has been found that the demands of the young readers require a more special treatment".[42] He advised specialised training, for it was "essential that the librarian should be so far acquainted with psychology as to appreciate the mental processes of the child"; and the best training preliminary to the technical (librarianship) training, he believed, was the Froebelian method.[43] This method, observed a contemporary of Sayers, William Benson Thorne, in 1918, "insisted

37 As explained by A. Van Slyck, *Free to all: Carnegie libraries and American culture 1890-1920* (Chicago: Chicago University Press, 1995), pp. 179-180.

38 G.S. Hall, 'The ideal school as based on child study', *Forum* [New York], Vol. 32 (September 1901), p. 39.

39 J.F. Soltis, 'Dewey, pragmatism and education', in *The International Encyclopedia of Education*, 2nd edition, Vol. 3 (Oxford: Elsevier, 1994), pp. 1520-1524.

40 C. Gustafsson, 'Montessori and education', in *The International Encyclopedia of Education*, 2nd edition, Vol. 7 (Oxford: Elsevier, 1994), pp. 3912-3914.

41 Sayers, *The children's library*, op. cit.

42 Ibid., pp. 73-74.

43 Ibid., pp. 196, 198.

on the need for drawing out the individual characteristics of each child, and relied on demonstration with practical objects and story telling".[44] Those working with children, said Sayers, "should become acquainted with their mental processes via the Froebelian method because of its power of understanding the imperfectly articulated conceptions of children".[45] Friedrich Froebel (1782-1852), founder of the 'kindergarten', believed children developed best through creative self-activity. Derived from his idealist belief, similar to that held by Jast, that the universe was an organism to which all other lesser organisms belonged, Froebel taught that the child was innately good and in order to realise its potential its development had to be 'natural' not 'prescriptive' or 'interfering'. The Froebel method emphasised free play, singing, group work, nature study, dance, outdoor activities and storytelling (the latter was not a feature of elementary schooling at the time).[46] The associated 'play way' educational method, developed by H. Caldwell Cook, was taken up in some London libraries in the 1920s.[47]

It is difficult to gauge the extent to which new ideas on education and child psychology influenced librarians and library designers and planners of the day. What is evident, however, is the similarities that existed between the discourses of educationalists and child psychologists and those concerned with providing children's libraries, including their architectural treatment. After the war Sayers inaugurated a children's department at Croydon, which he described lovingly in his *Manual of Children's Libraries* (1932). The room's colour scheme was worked out by the Borough Engineer's Department. The walls were decorated in glossy 'Spanish red', with upper layers of green and cream: an effect 'as utterly unofficial' as could be achieved.[48] Small bookcases and framed green baize screens were placed against the walls, and a large number of pictures were displayed. All doors and windows were curtained. A daïs (raised platform) at one end of the room, on which were placed tables and chairs, provided space for quiet reading, authorship and homework, and, of course, 'performance' activities; behind this daïs was a lantern screen which was covered with a velvet curtain when not in use (the daïs became a common

---

44   W.B. Thorne, 'Memorandum on Children's librarians', Library Association Library Development Committee (8 March 1918), Library Association Archives, University College London Archives Department.

45   Sayers, *The children's library*, op. cit., pp. 198.

46   J. Johansson, 'Froebel and education', in *The International Encyclopedia of Education*, 2nd edition, Vol. 4 (Oxford: Elsevier, 1994), pp. 2385-2388.

47   H.C. Cook, *The play way: an essay in educational method* (London: Heinemann, 1917).

48   Librarians and designers, as at Croydon, began to think hard about the colour format of the children's accommodation. Sayers, *A manual of children's libraries*, op. cit., p. 115, noted that in America one librarian suggested 'a cream-coloured wall, furniture finished in pearly grey and a large bowl of orange or deep blue placed conspicuously somewhere in the room to lend a bright note of colour'.

sight in later children's rooms). Reference books were placed proximate to the daïs. The centre of the room was filled with tables with an ample six-foot gangway between them. Tables could be folded away to allow the room to become a lecture or 'performance' space.[49] This was a place where children could not just come to read and be safe but to express themselves and engage in 'constructive play'.

Figure 2. The ideal children's library. Source: Gwendolyn Rees, *Libraries for Children* (London: Grafton, 1924), reprinted in W.B.C. Sayers, *A Manual of Children's Libraries* (London: Allen and Unwin, 1932).

In 1932 Sayers' *Manual* carried an idealised version of the children's room (originally published in 1924 in Gwendolen Rees' *Libraries for Children*).[50] It was a place in which children were in harmony with their surroundings. The décor was bright and lively and, above all, homely. The windows were curtained and the walls potted with pictures. A cosy fireplace and adjacent inglenook seating conveyed an impression of safety. Furniture was of a suitable size and appropriate to needs: tables for communal study and use of encyclopedic tomes, and bureaux for private study, perhaps homework. The relaxation experienced by the child was replicated in an easy relationship with the librarian over an unimposing desk. It might be suggested that this idealised place was conceptualised to a large degree as a feminised space, in keeping with the con-

49   Sayers, *A manual of children's libraries*, op. cit., pp. 106-107.
50   G. Rees, *Libraries for Children* (London: Grafton, 1924).

temporary discourse among librarians that women were best suited to work with children. It was not possible to replicate such an idealised image universally, or even perhaps widely, but some libraries did approach the ideal, the children's room at Croydon Central Library in the 1930s being a close example. In Manchester, Jast's young people's reading rooms set a new standard by categorically rejecting the schoolroom ambience and making use of flowers, pictures and low bookcases to soften the look.[51] Such environments had become not just surrogate homes for children – mere safe havens and shelters – but 'comfortable' homes away from home, evocative of 'middle-class domesticity'.

The practice of grafting the adult pattern of physical arrangements in the reading-room onto children's reading-rooms came under pressure from a new child-centred – or 'pedocentric', to use Hall's term – approach. The overriding consideration was to provide a home-like setting. Circular tables, which had begun to appear in children's rooms just before the First World War and now became much more common, mimicked the convivial family meal-time circle. Evocative of safety and warmth, the fireplace became the focal point of the children's room. Space was de-cluttered, encouraging greater freedom of movement and expression in a place where, henceforth, as Van Slyck notes in respect of American libraries, children would be allowed, within reason, to "tumble about"[52] (although in 1945 it was gleefully noted that children in the public library at Maghall "now *use* [original emphasis] the library instead of just grabbing a book, sliding around on the linoleum and being put outside").[53] Berwick Sayers believed that "it is well to have small separate writing-desks, or tables with divisions so arranged as to give each child as much privacy as possible. The chairs or seats should not be school forms, but should be comfortable, with backs to them".[54] Due to the fatigue as well as the noisy shuffling involved, children should not be forced to stand at reading slopes in the image of their adult counterparts.[55] However, at one of Nottingham's branches, as late as 1927, reading stands were provided so that children might "emulate their elders in the adjacent newsroom".[56]

Nonetheless, by this time Nottingham's Walter Briscoe was able to argue with increasing support that "future planning must be to cater for the requirements of the children first, and let adults take second place".[57] The juvenile room at the Withington Public Library, Manchester, which opened in 1927,

51   T. Kelly, *Books for the people: an illustrated history of the British public library* (London: Deutsch, 1977), p. 150. The rooms are described in Jast, *The child as reader*, op. cit., pp. 25-40.
52   Van Slyck, *Free to all*, op. cit., p. 186.
53   'Children's book week held at Maghall', *Library Association Record*, Vol. 47 (1945), p. 45.
54   Sayers, *The children's library*, op. cit., p. 100.
55   Sayers, *The children's library*, op. cit., p. 111.
56   Briscoe, *Library planning* (London: Grafton, 1927), p. 135.
57   Ibid., p. 138.

was proudly described by the authorities as "one of the most attractive departments of the library", and had a floor space equal to that of the main reading room.[58] Opened in the same year, the pleasant children's room at Nottingham's Southern Branch Library contained no desk-like reading tables, reminiscent of the schoolroom, but round tables with comfortable chairs suggestive of a children's club. Around the room are reading slopes, of a sit-to height, on which are more children's magazines and literature; and occasional settees, constructed for two, relieve the orthodoxy.[59]

At the Cross Gates (Percival Leigh) Public Library, Leeds in 1939 an interesting feature provided in the centre of the children's room was an electric fire surrounded by circular settees, a space principally designed for storytelling but also available for individual readers to use (reading circles and corners constructed by various kinds of furniture were a fairly common sight in inter-war children's room and were in many respects antecedents of the 'comfort zones' which were to appear later in the century and which are discussed below).[60] A further attractive feature of the room was a colourful mural depicting scenes from children's classics and inhabitants of various countries grouped around a map of the world. Pictures were said to inspire children, to give them an appreciation of art and provide an air of domesticity in the room. They could also convey messages, depending on the allegory of their content, of such things as courage, patriotism and the importance of reading and learning.[61] The children's department in the new Hillsborough Public Library, Sheffield (1929) was adorned by a large mural frieze painted by students from the local School of Art. In 1936 in the children's room at Scarborough Public Library four murals showing scenes from children's literature were painted by Scarborough-born artist Kenneth Rowntree.

The trend, therefore, was towards openness, comfort, intimacy and an elevation of children's tastes. At Sheepscar Branch Library in Leeds the junior room, as well as the adult lending library, were designed with "exceedingly attractive" low windows which were said to provide a "publicity value" and serve "to break up the monotonous run of shelving which mars the aesthetic appeal of so many library interiors".[62] Planners began to question the "obses-

58   City of Manchester Public Libraries, *A note on the new building of the Withington Public Library* (1927).

59   Briscoe, *Library planning*, op. cit., p. 135.

60   Leeds Libraries and Arts Committee, *Official opening of the Percival Leigh [Cross Gates] Public Library* (1939). 'A new library at Cross Gates, Leeds', *National Builder*, Vol. 19, No. 6 (January 1940), p. 155. J.T. Gillet, 'Percival Leigh Branch Library, Cross Gates, Leeds', *Library Association Record*, Vol. 42 (February 1940), p. 41.

61   Briscoe, *Library planning*, op. cit., p. 136.

62   J.T. Gillet, 'Sheepscar Branch Library, Leeds', *Library Association Record*, Vol. 40 (August 1938), p. 413.

sion with the fetish of supervision" in children's rooms.[63] The changing approach to children's library design reflected a growing trust in the child reader.

1945–1980: Open-plan and modern office

After the Second World War children's libraries continued to be developed as a major aspect of public library provision, which itself benefited considerably from the growth of a welfare state and, once the austerity years of the post-war era had passed, of public expenditure also. In 1947 the Association of Children's Librarians, formed a decade earlier, officially joined the Library Association (working alongside a Youth Libraries Section) and by 1959 boasted a thousand members.[64] In the mid-1950s a shortage of trained children's librarians was identified and some training was put in place to remedy the problem.[65]

It is true that in the immediate post-war period a whiff of Victorianism could still be found in the views of the children's library held by some: in 1951 the librarian Charles Elliot wrote of the "ephemeral atrocities that shame the shelves of many juvenile libraries".[66] Librarians often saw the children's library as a cultural battlefield where the tide of corrosive popular culture – whether in the form of 'opiate' literature, comic books, television or library-based puppet shows – could be turned back.[67] Librarians identified a link between the horror comic and juvenile delinquency.[68] "Let the libraries introduce the children to the book before they become addicts of the comic strip", wrote one librarian in 1952.[69] However, from the 1960s onwards a more liberal and constructive tone to children's library work, building on the advances of the 1920s and 1930s, became apparent: in 1963, for example, the President of the Scottish School Libraries Association argued that comics had "done far more good than harm".[70] With the assistance of a new Library Association syllabus

---

63 Ibid.

64 Ellis, *Library services for young people*, op. cit., p. 98.

65 J. Butler, 'Survey of public library services for children', *Library Association Record*, Vol. 57 (1955), p. 450-451. In 1955 a six-week full-time course on library work for young people was provided by the North-Western Polytechnic in London, as advertised in the *Library Association Record*, Vol. 57 (1955), p. 322.

66 C.A. Elliott, *Library publicity and service* (London: Grafton, 1951), p. 63.

67 J.D. Reynolds, *Library buildings, 1965* (London: Library Association, 1966), p. 7 carries a photograph of children reading poetry in the public library in Kirkby, Liverpool. In a patronising fashion, the photograph's caption tells us that "the community is rough and tough, but children read poetry in Kirkby", implying that children's consumption of 'traditional' literature, even in a 'rough and tough area', was what librarians mostly wished to see.

68 F. Wertham, 'Seduction of the innocent', *Library Association Record*, Vol. 57 (1955), p. 170.

69 S. Uniechowska, 'Libraries and the pre-school child', *Library Association Record*, Vol. 54 (1952), p. 365.

70 'Gobbledegook – or "pleasant conceit"', *Liaison: The News-Sheet of the Library Association* (August 1963), p. 53.

and the introduction of two-year training courses in library schools, both encouraging specialisation in professional preparation, a thoroughly "professional approach", as Ellis put it, emerged.[71] Young children, those under 7 or 8, were more actively encouraged. The growing interest in services to children was seen elsewhere too, as reflected in the establishment in 1955 of the Committee on Library Work with Children and Young People organised under the banner of the International Federation of Library associations (IFLA).

Until the late 1950s the economic climate did not allow the resumption of public library construction, but thereafter, until the mid-1970s, investment in the physical infrastructure of the public library mushroomed. The growing openness towards the child reader that was evident before 1939 continued after the war and found expression in a move towards open planning in architecture, including design for the home, a sphere from which the children's library had drawn a good deal of its design inspiration between the wars. The shift towards open plan marked a significant break in the design history of the children's library, and so some discussion of its origins and early development is appropriate at this juncture.

Open plan design (sometimes called 'free plan' or 'fluid plan') was a new vision of architectural space born at the beginning of the twentieth century, though with roots also in the late-nineteenth-century vogue for Japanese design connected with the Arts-and-Crafts Movement. It was made possible by new construction techniques (especially reinforced concrete) that eliminated the need for interior load-bearing walls. Beyond technology, the open plan was furthered, as Adi Shamir Zion has argued, by parallel developments in science and culture – from Freud's "fluid scape" of the unconscious mind and Einstein's new way of looking at the time-space relationship, to the free and natural choreography of the American dancer Isadora Duncan and the free expression of Picasso's cubist shapes. Architects began to break free from traditional and spatial constraints. This was most visibly seen in the realm of house design. The open plan was a critical ingredient in Frank Lloyd Wright's prairie houses (e.g. the Robie House, 1910). The elimination of self-contained rooms was also a feature of Le Corbusier's (e.g. Villa Savoye, 1929), a house hollowed out in every direction, representing what he and contemporaries such as Mies van der Rohe (e.g. Tugendhat House, 1930) termed "le plan libre". Free-flowing floor plans were later combined with large expanses of glass wall that at once replaced windows and blurred the distinction between inside and outside.[72] Large expanses of glass could also mitigate the smallness of a house, delivering compactness with the illusion of spaciousness.[73] After the Second World War,

---

71   Ellis, *Library services for young people*, pp. 119-167.
72   A.S. Zion, *Open house: unbound space and the modern dwelling* (New York: Rizzoli International Publications, 2002).
73   S. Isenstadt, *The modern American house: spaciousness and middle-class identity* (Cambridge: Cambridge University Press, 1975), p. 175.

open plan also became a feature of the large office block. Post-war modernism saw the emergence of the 'open office' with floor space broken up by fabric-covered screens, desks, filing cabinets, plants and other 'barrier' devices. Layout was defined by traffic flow rather than rigidly defined work hierarchies.[74]

In the school context, open plan was pioneered by Francis O'Neill, head teacher of Prestolee School, Lancashire, between 1918 and 1953. Francis believed children learnt by doing (his school became known as the "learn by doing school") and did so at their own individual pace (self-generated learning). The critical design innovation he implemented was the conversion of the assembly hall into an open plan classroom. The room was accessible to pupils of all ages. Screens and other furniture provided necessary and flexible zoning and long tables were grouped together to provide large flat areas for activities in small groups. This arrangement flew in the face of half a century of school design, articulated most loudly by E.R. Robson and his work for the London School Board, which organised age-related classrooms around an assembly hall, a system which had first been developed in Prussia and which contradicted starkly the older method of simultaneous teaching of all ages in one large space.[75] In some respects, therefore, the O'Neill formula was a throwback to the first half of the nineteenth century and earlier; as was the trend in the 1960s and 1970s, especially in primary education, towards open-plan schools which were characterised by a large floor-plate to enhance flexibility; open classrooms; movable furnishings used as class partitions; and spatial continuity between classroom and circulation space.[76]

Open-plan learning was further encouraged, in Britain and elsewhere, by the example of the infant-toddler centres and pre-schools of Reggio Emilia in Northern Italy, inspired by the childcare specialist Loris Malaguzzi. The Reggio Emilia programme of early childhood education, started in 1945, went on to gain an international reputation. The Reggio Emilia approach recognises the environment as the 'third teacher' – parents and carers being the first two. Great attention is given to the look and feel of the early-years setting. Space is organised for small and large group projects and small intimate spaces for one, two or three children. Displays are at both adult and children's eye level and the furniture is designed to be multifunctional. Reggio settings make marked use of natural and artificial light, with floor to ceiling windows and pale walls that offset the colourful artwork done by the children. An important design feature of the Reggio Emilia institutions was an internal central square, or

---

74 A. Massey, *Interior design in the twentieth century*, 2nd edition (London: Thames and Hudson, 2001), p. 146.

75 M. Dudek, *Schools and kindergartens: a design manual* (Basel and Boston: Birkhäuser, 2008), pp. 10-15.

76 A. Van Slyck, 'School', in *Encyclopedia of 20th-century architecture* (London: Routledge, 2004), p. 1181.

piazza. This was a public meeting place for the school conceptualised in the tradition of the outdoor town piazza.[77]

Given the strong twentieth-century evolutionary history of the open plan in architecture – whether in the home or the office – it is not surprising to see the adoption of open-plan design in the library setting coinciding with the rampant design modernism of the 1950s and 1960s. The take-up of open plan was especially enthusiastic in Scandinavia where, as the Danish librarian Sven Plovgaard explained on a visit to Britain in 1960, it was believed that sharply defined departments gave an impression of an institution-like library (though in very large libraries some departmentalisation was inevitable); whereas open interiors made for an informal, flexible and efficient plan, any separate spacing needed being manufactured by careful arrangement of furniture and various moveable barriers.[78] When a new central library for Birmingham was being planned in the 1960s, the open-plan system was advocated because it was thought that it would "give the building a longer useful life by making it possible to adapt and re-distribute space to meet changes in requirements and activities as the years go by".[79]

The strengthening of the open-plan philosophy after the Second World War in the context of the home was driven by an enthusiasm for technological advances as well as a poetic desire on the part of society to break loose from an oppressive era of depression and war. It also symbolised a concern for the welfare of children and a desire to give them greater freedom.[80] Arguably, this impulse leeched over into the planning of children's libraries. Open plan buildings allowed children's library services to become more integrated into the general work and image of the library; and in the 1960s and 1970s it became extremely common. In 1960, in the renovated Ormeau Road Branch Library in Belfast, one-third of the space was given over to the children's accommodation but there was no physical partition between the area used by children and that used by adults (though the children's section was demarcated by a lower ceiling).[81] By 1965, small libraries at Nine Elms (South-West London), Mountsorrel (Leicestershire) and Selsey (West Sussex) had been designed to provide a free flow of space between children's and adults' sections, although there were certainly continuing examples of entirely separate accommodation also – as at the Brookhill Road Library, East Barnet where enclosed junior reference and

---

77   Dudek, *Schools and kindergartens*, op. cit., pp. 10-15.
78   S. Plovgaard, 'Building layout in Denmark', in K.M. Newbury (ed.), *Design in the library* (Penge: The Library Association London and Home Counties Branch, 1960), pp. 20-21.
79   '£2¼ million open-plan project for Birmingham's new central', *Liaison: News-Sheet of the Library Association* (February 1963), p. 10.
80   C.A. Pearson (ed.), *Modern American houses: fifty years of design in the 'Architectural Record'*, 2nd edition (New York: Harry N. Abrams and the Architectural Record, 2005), p. 15.
81   I.A. Crawley, Belfast: Ormeau Road Branch, *Library Association Record*, Vol. 62 (1960), p. 346.

lending rooms were placed on the first floor, separate from the adult reference section (also on the first floor) and the adult lending section downstairs; and at Hornsey Central Library, which not only had a separate room for juniors but also a separate entrance, representing a throwback to the Victorian era).[82] 'Skilful designing', gave children at Eastbourne's new central library "a distinct library of their own but [one] which is not actually separated from the main library"; the transition was said to have been "effected naturally and with the minimum of break".[83]

The lowering of barriers between adult and child accommodation was not appropriate everywhere. In Pimlico, in London's Westminster district, a standalone children's library was opened in 1960 (due to the heavy road traffic and the large number of non-residential areas in Westminster the best place for an adult service was not always the best place for a children's service).[84] The library occupied two shop units at the base of a seven-storey block of flats on the edge of the Churchill Gardens Housing Estate. The library's internal design was uncompromisingly modern. A ceiling of deal 'tongue and grooved' boards treated with a plastic matt sealer was complemented by flooring in polished maple and plastered walls painted blue and light grey. All unpainted wooden fixtures and fittings were in West African hardwood. To avoid clutter, no freestanding bookcases were supplied, the two display cases that occupied floor space being fitted with wheels to facilitate movement. The staff counter was of "a novel light design in metal and glass". The L-shaped room was lit on its two inner sides by natural light from a glass-screened courtyard which served as an outdoor reading room in the summer months. Photographs of the room reveal a highly contemporary interior design, with a modernist simplicity typical of the time. From the photographic evidence alone, however, one cannot tell that the room was the site of a children's library service. Its appearance is more like that of the modern office. Indeed, a great many children's libraries of the 1960s appear to take their cue from the office environment, providing workmanlike tables alongside more comfortable furniture.[85]

The instigator of the Pimlico Children's Library was Lionel McColvin, Librarian of Westminster and the leading professional librarian of his day. His thoughts on children's libraries were extensively publicised in his book *Libraries for children* (1961), the front cover of which carried a photograph of the Pimlico library. Drawing on the practices of his Victorian professional forebears, he

---

82   See plans or photographs of these libraries in the *Library Association Record*, Vol. 66 (1964), pp. 541, 567, 568, 572; and in Reynolds, *Library buildings, 1965*, op. cit., p. 45.

83   'Eastbourne's new Central Library', *Library Association Record*, Vol. 66 (1964), p. 520.

84   The description that follows is in L.R. McColvin, 'Pimlico Children's Library', *Library Association Record*, Vol. 62 (1960), pp. 367-368.

85   The term 'workmanlike tables' was used in connection with the children's reference collection at Hornsey Public Library in the mid-1960s, as reported by Reynolds, *Library buildings, 1965*, op. cit., p. 44.

Figure 3. Source: Lionel McColvin, *Libraries for Children* (London: Phoenix House, 1961).

advised that the children's room should be made to look as much like the adult library as possible, only "cosier and more opulent";[86] or as he put it on another occasion, the children's department should be a "shade smarter than

---

86   L.R. McColvin, *Libraries for children* (London: Phoenix House, 1961), p. 120.

the others".[87] He urged that children's libraries should avoid the schoolroom look and protested that too many still looked out-dated, "bare and heavy, with clumsy old-fashioned furniture and the type of decoration which might be appropriate to a public lavatory or a railway station" and perhaps scarred by "over-powering murals" and "silly mock ingle-nooks".[88] In design terms, as in many other aspects of library policy and provision, McColvin was an avowed moderniser. Following a visit to Finland in 1957 he exclaimed that: "They are ahead of us"; Britain needed to start re-building and improving its libraries, "or we will soon be living in the past", he warned.[89] The Scandinavian treatment of children's accommodation *in particular* also found favour among British librarians.[90]

For McColvin, as for many of his contemporaries, children's libraries needed to embrace the modernist revolution in design, even if that meant a synchronisation with adult accommodation and the adoption of a ubiquitous, minimalist style. The library literature of the 1960s is replete with images of children's libraries subjected to the modernist design ethos of the day. In 1964 at Brentford and Chiswick Central library, the children's room was dramatically transformed from a dull, cluttered pre-war space into a brightly lit, spacious facility sporting sleek Scandinavian furniture.[91] At times, the most striking feature of the modernist children's library appeared to be its sparseness, as evident in the young reader's corner in Feltham Public Library.[92]

After 1980: Domestic 'comfort zone' and pop culture playground

Against a backdrop of economic turbulence and an associated growth of political radicalism, in the 1970s and 1980s a new mode of public library service emerged and spread in Britain: community librarianship.[93] Its aim, not shared by the entire library community, it has to be said, was to prioritise the 'disadvantaged' by de-institutionalising the public library and moving services outside the walls of the library and into the community. By re-locating themselves

87   L.R. McColvin, *British libraries* (London: Longmans, Green and Co. for the British Council, 1946), p. 23.

88   McColvin, *Libraries for children*, op. cit., p. 121.

89   L.R. McColvin, 'A visit to Finland', *Library Association Record*, Vol. 59 (1957), p. 296.

90   H. Jones and L. Medlock, 'Children's libraries in Scandinavia: first impressions', *Library Review*, Vol. 22, No. 5 (1970), pp. 251-254.

91   P. Millard, *Modern library equipment* (London: Crosby Lockwood, 1966), pp. 41-42.

92   Photograph in Reynolds, *Library buildings, 1965*, op. cit., p. 47.

93   A. Black and D.Muddiman, *Understanding community librarianship: the public library in postmodern Britain* (Aldershot: Avebury Press, 1997). W. Martin, *Library services to the disadvantaged* (London: Bingley, 1975).

deep inside the community, it was argued, librarians could open up library services and make them 'community catalysts'.[94] This new focus entailed the targeting of specific client groups, a strategy that proved beneficial to users and potential users of the children's library. The title of Janet Hill's 1973 book on children's library services, *Children are people: the librarian in the community*,[95] reflected a new determination to improve services by rationally identifying the reading, cultural and information needs of the young and recognising that these needs were substantially different from those of adult users.

One of the legacies of this new way of looking at children's provision was the appearance in places of strategies and separate spaces for teenagers,[96] a trend underpinned by the inexorable rise of 'youth culture', which was sustained not only by the widening gap between the end of childhood and the beginning of adulthood but also by a distinctive pattern of peer-group leisure consumption and a concern with style.[97] The first dedicated teenage library had appeared in Walthamstow in the 1930s. In 1962, the librarian Gordon Bearman suggested that library books for youths could be placed in the canteens of further education colleges and that mobile libraries could serve youth clubs in the evening.[98] In 1964 Hertfordshire County Council started to issue a series of leaflets called 'Teenread', partly in an effort to encourage teenagers to buy paperback books for themselves.[99] However, little real progress was made in this area until the 1980s, the problem of providing materials for teenagers often simply being negotiated by providing two collections for the group, one in the adult library, one in the children's library.[100] In the 1980s a clutch of teenage libraries appeared around Glasgow, for example: the Castlemilk Teenager Library, the Johnstone Information and Leisure Library and the Yoker Teenage Library.[101] In 1985 the Xchange teenage room was opened in Bradford Central Library in response to a growing ethnic population and rising teenage unemployment. The majority of users were in the age range 13-17, but 11% of

94 A.M. Adams, 'How to "open" a library', *Library Association Record*, Vol. 75 (1973), pp. 152-153.

95 J. Hill, *Children are people: the librarian in the community* (London: Hamilton, 1973).

96 L. Love, 'Teenagers and library use in Waltham Forest', *Library Association Record*, Vol. 89 (1987), pp. 81-82.

97 'Youth culture', in S. Bruce and S. Yearley (eds.), *The Sage dictionary of sociology* (London: Sage, 2006).

98 H.G.K. Bearman, 'Literacy, libraries and youth', in *Book provision for special needs* (London: Library Association London and Home Counties Branch, 1962), pp. 35-36.

99 S.G. Ray, 'Library work with children and young people', in P.H. Sewell (ed.), *Five years' work in librarianship 1961-1965* (London: Library association, 1968), p. 380.

100 D. Denham, 'Public library services for children', in A. Black and P. Hoare (eds.), *The Cambridge history of libraries in Britain and Ireland. Volume 3: 1850-2000* (Cambridge: Cambridge University Press, 2006), pp. 108-109.

101 A. Miller, 'Notes from abroad: a study tour of German libraries', *Library Association Record*, Vol. 91 (1989), p. 224.

users were in their 20s. The design of the library was said to be "upmarket and trendy, using bright and sophisticated furnishings ... aiming to create an atmosphere somewhere between a bookshop and a coffee shop".[102]

If teenage library provision was a prime concern in the 1980s, the 1990s and beyond were marked by a shift in children's library services towards the very young. This increased interest in the very young child and her family has impacted considerably on the services provided by libraries and on children's library design. Early childhood is now high on the political agenda with children's services receiving a high profile as policymakers are concerned about social malaise, education and the level of reading skills in the information age. During the last decade, the UK's Labour government has viewed the way out of poverty to be through education and a high level of literacy, and has committed considerable funding to targeting 'effective' early childhood education and care. Initiatives have been launched to encourage parents to enter and remain in paid work, supported by better childcare provisions and more flexible employment. The 'United Kingdom Millennium Cohort'[103] study provides an opportunity to reflect on the circumstances of children in Britain at the start of a new century. In previous generations mothers generally stayed away from paid work while they had young children; since 1980 there have been very large increases in labour force participation of mothers with pre-school children, doubling over 20 years. There has been a major expansion in pre-school education over the last 30 or so years. The proportion of three and four year olds enrolled in all schools in the UK rose from 21 % in 1970-71 to 65% in 2003-04. Inter-professional and inter-agency working are important features of initiatives such as the Sure Start Local Programmes for young children, set up to address social exclusion in local communities through a multi-disciplinary team approach.

In the past, public library services mainly focused on children who already knew how to read. Public libraries in the UK are now actively encouraging parents and carers of babies and very young children to join in language and literacy activities; while IFLA, in its *Guidelines for library services to babies and toddlers* (2007), focuses on meeting the needs of families with children under three, which means, amongst other things, providing "an accessible, inviting, attractive, safe, non-challenging and non-threatening place to visit ... [where there are] no barriers to access, like steps without elevators, or heavy doors, or areas which might be unsafe for crawling and toddling youngsters".[104]

---

102   J. Nicholson and H. Pain-Lewis, 'The teenage library in Bradford: an evaluation of exchange', *Journal of Librarianship*, Vol. 20, No. 3 (July 1998), p. 206.

103   Dex, S. and Joshi, H. (eds) *Children of the 21ˢᵗ Century: from birth to nine months* (Bristol: The Polity Press, 2005) [Part of the UK Millennium Cohort Study Series].

104   International Federation of Library Associations (IFLA), *Guidelines for library services to babies and toddlers* (The Hague: IFLA, 2007) [IFLA Professional Reports No. 100], p. 7.

In 2002 a working group from the Chartered Institute of Library and Information Professionals (CILIP) provided an overview of library services to children and young people in a report titled *Start with the child*. Arguing that libraries can change children's lives, the report also praised the emergence of partnership initiatives, such as those where library authorities have worked closely with the Sure Start schemes inaugurated in 1997, the aim of which are to deliver the best start in life for every child by bringing together early-years education, childcare, health and family support. Many library authorities in Sure Start areas have succeeded in gaining funding for early-years workers and libraries are also involved as partners in delivering the Bookstart[105] national programme that encourages all parents and carers to enjoy books with their children from as early an age as possible. Bookstart aims to provide a free pack of books to every baby in the UK. Libraries, health professionals and early-years professionals give the packs to the parents and carers with an invitation to visit the local library.

Thinking carefully about designing for early-years services generally is certainly not new,[106] but in recent years considerable energy has been expended in the area, including the library field. In Wakefield, Sure Start has funded the Sunshine Library, the first designated early-years library in the country.[107] The innovative Sunshine Library, located in a community centre on the Lupset Housing Estate, opened in 2001. Designed with the help of parents and by removing traditional barriers it became a key social space in the local area. The Sunshine Library was purpose-built to support early language development and book enjoyment among families living in a deprived community. Communities give purpose to libraries and local families were actively involved throughout the planning and development of the Sunshine Library and were consulted during the drafting of the plans. They helped to select book stock, furniture and equipment. They were involved in choosing the farmyard theme for the library interior and the 'Sunshine' name for the library.[108]

Running alongside the concern to improve the life chances of the very young, there has also emerged a focus on the family and the need to develop policies to strengthen family life. In recent years, the image of a 'broken Britain' has gained currency. To a large degree it has done so by virtue of escalating

---

105 http://www.bookstart.org.uk/ [viewed September 2011].

106 Matrix and the Greater London Council Women's Committee, *Buildings for childcare: making better buildings for the under-5s* (London, 1986).

107 Chartered Institute of Library and Information Professionals (CILIP), *Start with the child: report of the CILIP Working Group on Library Provision for Children and Young People* (London: CILIP, 2002), p. 39.

108 C. Rankin et al., *The role of the early years librarian in developing an information community: a case study of effective partnerships and early years literacy within a Sure Start project in Wakefield*, Proceedings of the 35th Annual Conference of the Canadian Association of Information Science, Montreal (2007).

concern – commencing as a 'fin de siècle' anxiety – about care in the family, domestic violence, lone parenting, the selfish individualism of absent fathers and the future of marriage as an institution.[109] In response to the perception of the multiple toxic consequences of family breakdown, in 1997 the Labour Government established a 'Ministerial Group on the Family' and announced its intention to develop strategies that would increase support for family life.[110] The *Every child matters* (2003) consultation Green Paper was part of the Government's response to the inquiry into the horrific murder, by her guardians, of Victoria Climbié and outlined plans to improve the services supporting children from all backgrounds, looking at how such a framework could protect those most at risk. The longitudinal research programme 'The Effective Provision of Pre-School Education' (EPPE) demonstrated the importance of parents in children's early educational achievement, showing that what parents and carers do makes a real difference.[111]

Recently, the library community in the UK has forcefully argued that encouraging young children and their families to access a library can provide a good foundation not only for developing early literacy but also for supporting the family as an ingredient of social stability. The importance of the family was also recognised by IFLA in its *Guidelines for Children's Library Services* published in 2003.[112] It is now seen as important to make information available to parents to encourage them to bring their child to the library (something which contrasts vividly with children's library use in earlier generations when, as the photographic evidence confirms, children, albeit juniors rather than infants, went to the library alone). The library is promoted as a community hub – welcoming all. Library managers are working to ensure that traditional barriers to access and use are broken down and removed. If parents and carers are relaxed and made to feel welcome, this enhances the experience for all and should lead to repeat visits to the library.

In the 1990s, the community librarianship approach described above gave way to the less contentious discourse of 'social inclusion': policies – including those in the areas of child welfare, the family, education and public libraries – that would address the social exclusion that accompanied and reinforced poverty. In addressing social and economic deprivation, policy makers became interested in the concept of 'social capital', this being the construction of what

109 J. Lewis, 'Family change and lone parents as a social problem', in M. May, R. Page and E. Brunsdon (eds.), *Understanding social problems: issues in social policy* (Oxford: Blackwell, 2001), pp. 37-54.

110 Ministerial Group on the Family, *Supporting families: a consultation document* (London: Stationery Office, November 1998).

111 K. Sylva et al., *The effective provision of pre-school education [EPPE] Project: final Report* (London: DFES/Institute of Education, University of London, 2004).

112 IFLA Libraries for Children and Young Adults Section, *Guidelines for Children's Library Services* (2003).

one might call a 'social infrastructure', the building of active connections between people based on mutual understanding and trust as well as shared values and behaviours. Arising out of the social capital discourse came the suggestion that greater attention should be paid to '*physical* capital', the very structure and nature of the places and spaces we are creating. A recent study by the market research organisation MORI has demonstrated the impact of the built environment on our quality of life, where homes, schools, doctor's surgeries, streets and parks combine to form the 'physical capital' of a location.[113] The premise is that concerns about improving quality of life should focus more attention on the design quality of the urban fabric.[114]

In keeping with these ideas, it has been recognised that libraries can help to build social capital by providing physical capital in the form of a safe place for people to meet, socialise and relax. One of the major developments in domestic interior design in recent years has been the idea of the *comfort zone*, reflecting our propensity for 'cocooning' (stay-at-home lifestyle) as a reaction to what some see as a time of social anxiety and public behaviour and morals: "Staying in with a book – the new going out" is how one librarian has put it recently.[115] As part of this trend, 'lounging' in the home has become a style of entertainment.[116] The sanctuary function of the home has grown significantly, as reflected in the boast of IKEA, the giant Scandinavian retailer of high-styled, mid-priced furniture, that it isn't simply a business but also "a way of life".[117] Design for the home as comfort zone and sanctuary has influenced the design of some public spaces, such as bookstores and coffee shops. Domestic influences on public-space design have also been evident in libraries, which have been re-styled as 'living rooms in the city'.[118] The children's library has clearly absorbed these domestic design tendencies, reflecting the concern for the family, and especially young children, noted above. In Denmark, it is interesting to note, some librarians have been taking advice directly from IKEA.[119]

However, to view the contemporary children's library as a 'public sphere' space representing a valuable stock of social capital – as 'haven' from a materialistic, individualistic and morally diseased society – runs counter to the way

---

113   Ipsos MORI, *Physical capital: liveability in 2005* (2005).

114   C. Rankin and A. Brock, *Delivering the best start: a guide to early years libraries* (London: Facet Publishing, 2009), p. 58.

115   S. Mckenzie, 'Staying in with a book – the new going out', *Library and Information Update* (May 2009), p. 29.

116   S.J. Slotkis, *Foundations of interior design* (London: Lawrence King), p. 408.

117   B. Torekull, *Leading by design: the IKEA story* (New York: Harper Business, 1999).

118   K. Worpole, *21st century libraries: changing forms, changing futures* (CABE [Commission for Architecture and the Built Environment], April 2004), p. 12.

119   M.C. Madsen, 'Denmark: the room as mediator: interview with project manager', *Scandinavian Public Library Quarterly*, Vol. 41, No. 3 (2008): http://splq.info/issues/vol41_3/08.htm [viewed September 2011].

its image has been shaped by the growth of commercialised popular culture and family-focused leisure. While it is true that children's libraries have reflected design trends in the domestic interior, they have also chimed with patterns of family consumption in popular culture, from McDonald's to Disney. Just as in the sphere of the McDonald's hamburger chain, food (sometimes accompanied by free toys) is seen as entertainment and the restaurant as play area,[120] so also in the environment of the children's library the semiotics of its design components has to a large degree been that of *playground* – the reading and educational equivalent of fast-food restaurant.[121] In aping the McDonald's playground look, the children's library might be seen to be buying into restaurant's status as a signifier of modernity, social relevance and contemporary appeal.

A classic recent example of the children's library as playground is that provided in the Aarhus Public Library, Denmark, where a child-centred focus means that the 'Children's Interactive Library' project actively involved children in designing multimedia library services, identifying what a library would have to provide so that the young can learn to interact and communicate through a combination of play, learning and physical activity.[122] In another Scandinavian example, The Mars Express[123] concept was developed in three county libraries in Sweden between 2005-2008, with a focus on listening to children and young people. The first phase developed and tested methods to get children actively engaged in the design and purpose of the library's physical spaces; the second phase explored how new technology could help develop a library environment conducive to creativity, learning, play and fantasy. Also based on the development needs of children, the Library of 100 Talents in Heerhugowaard[124] is part of the 2040 Libraries project of the Netherlands, which is aiming to design the public library of the future in as imaginative a way as possible. The concept finds its roots in the educational vision of Reggio Emilia (discussed above) where children design their own learning environment.

Continuing this line of thought, and noting that the term 'McDonaldisation' is primarily evocative of rationalization, efficiency, Fordism and scien-

---

120   H. Brembeck, 'Inscribing Nordic childhoods at McDonald's', in M. Gutman and N. De Conick-Smith (eds.), *Designing modern childhoods: history, space and the material culture of children* (Rutgers University Press, 2008), pp. 269-281.

121   J.L. Kincheloe, *The sign of the burger: McDonald's and the culture of power* (Philadelphia: Temple University Press, 2002), p. 89.

122   http://www.e-architect.co.uk/aarhus/jpgs/aarhus_library_shl050309_4.jpg [viewed September 2011].

123   L. Clasesson, The key to future libraries for children and young people *Scandanavian Public Library Quarterly* No 3, (2008) pp. 10-11.

124   M. Mosch and K. Bertrams, 'Library of 100 Talents – Heerhugowaard, Netherlands', Session 103: Libraries for Children and Young Adults, and Library Buildings and Equipment. World Library and Information Congress: 75th IFLA General Conference and Assembly (Milan, 24th August 2009).

tific management,[125] yet in a world rich in post-modern forms, the concept of 'Disneyisation' may be more appropriate for our analysis. Disney theme park culture is heterogeneous, but its central signifier is arguably the cartoon, one of the most popular and technologically interesting media advances of the twentieth century. It is not only the vivid colours and cartoon-like exaggerated details of the Disney theme parks and resorts (as seen in 'Mickey's Toontown or Orlando's 'All-Star and Pop-Century Hotels)[126] that may have in places found their way into the design of the children's library, emphasising again its function as 'playground'; it is also the concept that is situated at the core of the Disney experience: 'theming'. Theming – in this context the use of a design 'narrative' that is consciously imposed on a particular space or physical environment – is now used as a part of a strategy of differentiation by service providers as diverse as restaurants, shopping malls, zoos and museums. It may be spreading, as Bryman has noted, "not just because service providers and others perceive it to be a weapon for getting money out of our pockets", but also because "it has a kind of multiplier or snowball effect in our consciousness: we increasingly expect the accoutrements of theming".[127] Maximea[128] has argued that the design of themed museum exhibition spaces has been influenced over the last few decades by the development of commercial themed experiences. In particular, in many museums there has been an adaptation of techniques borrowed from the Disney theme parks. These developments have increased public familiarity with, and expectations of, large scale exhibition spaces that have the capability to present technically challenging exhibitry. In addition, new children's museums are opening every day, again with an emphasis as much on play as on learning. There is a growing trend for museums of all types to include a children's discovery room or a children's gallery, a key ingredient here, and increasingly in museums generally, being the active or interactive element.

An early example of theming in libraries was that included in the Waterthorpe Community Library, Sheffield in the late-1980s. Here, in the children's section, a story booth with sound system was constructed in the form of a medieval castle, outside the entrance to which a large plastic dragon, on which children could sit and climb, was positioned.[129] Recent themed designs include those at public libraries in Oswestry (castle), Sutton (jungle) and Folkstone (starry sky), photographic examples of which can be accessed via the on-line

125   A. Bryman, *The Disneyization of society* (Sage Publishers, 2004), p. 13.

126   B. Dunlop, *Building a dream: the art of Disney architecture* (New York: Abrams, 1996), pp. 180-189.

127   Bryman, *The Disneyization of society*, op. Cit., p. 53.

128   H. Maximea, 'Exhibition galleries', in B. Lord and G.D. Lord (eds.), *The manual of museum exhibitions* (Altamira Press, 2002), pp. 143-195.

129   A. Woodfoffe, 'Waterthorpe: Sheffield's new flagship community library', *Library Association Record*, Vol. 91, No. 8 (1989), p. 463.

Designing Libraries Gallery.[130] The Sunshine Library in Wakefield, described above, has a farmyard look. It was designed by a company called 'Animania!', which specialises in producing themed environments for children not only in libraries but in hospitals, museums and schools also.[131]

Figure 4. The Sunshine Library, Wakefield. Source: Carolynn Rankin

A further prime example of the themed space in connection with the children's library is in the exciting, interactive, re-modelled space named 'The Trove'[132] in White Plains Public Library, New York, opened in 2005 (the building itself is a late-modernist structure dating from 1974). The aim of the makeover was to re-create the library for a new generation that is used to being entertained, engaged and active. The planners and designers looked at museums, playgrounds and bookstores for ideas. Planning the project took several years. The library staff decided what they wanted for the children and worked with a team of other professionals: architects, theatrical designers and lighting specialists. The Trove provides different environments and experiences for children from birth through to the age of about eleven. The name was suggested by a brand-

---

130   Designing Libraries Gallery, http://www.designinglibraries.org.uk/gallery/main.php [viewed October 2011].
131   http://www.animania.org.uk/Animania%20Libraries.html [viewed October 2011].
132   http://thetrove.org/ [viewed October 2011].

ing firm based on the idea that a 'trove' is a collection of valuable items discovered or found. The Trove is a multisensory, multimedia space which is entered through a jagged brick opening in the wall on the library's second floor – a motif for the traditional library blown apart! The Compass is the focal point of The Trove and serves a number of purposes – information, reference, assistance with circulation and printing. Each of the environments in The Trove is very different. The areas closest to the opening are for older children while areas for younger children are deeper inside the complex where it is more contained and intimate.

Themed, fantasy design typifies the tendency towards post-modern hyper-reality, countering the rationalism and realism of the modern. This is not to say, however, that there has been a complete break with the modernism that delivered the open-plan, office-like children's library of earlier decades. Modernism lives on in interior design in terms of the high-tech or industrial feel, incorporating such elements as modern technology, factory-style flooring and steel scaffolding, staircases, pillars and roof girders – the type of look one can perhaps find references to in the Idea Stores of East London, libraries rebranded as such by the Borough of Tower Hamlets [133] while modernist minimalism is now re-packaged as Chinese 'Feng Shui' – the organisation of interior spaces around Zen principles. [134]

Conclusion

The public children's library in Britain is little over a century old. During that time its design is something in which librarians have taken a keen and persistent interest. The history of children's library design is marked by four identifiable phases. As a new cultural phenomenon with no architectural precedent to follow, children's libraries before the First World War not surprisingly drew on the design format of the schoolroom, with its ordered rows of forward-facing desks, tables and chairs and its disciplined, sterile ambience. This 'school-shelter' format corresponded to early motives behind children's library provision centred on the need to safeguard the moral fibre of the nation's young, to rescue children from the degradation and dangers of the streets and to build a healthy population that could help strengthen Britain economically and imperially.

The design of the children's library after 1918 mirrors an increasingly liberal approach to children's library provision, contrasting with the stereotype of control and repression which has been attached to pre-modern provision. As

---

133 http://www.ideastore.co.uk/ [viewed September 2011].

134 A. Massey, *Interior design in the twentieth century*, 2nd edition (London: Thames and Hudson, 2001), p. 168.

attitudes to childhood changed and as children began to receive greater attention from child welfare experts and greater protection from the state (something which had begun to happen before the war), the formal, sombre ambience of children's rooms began to give way to brighter, domestic settings, of the kind seen in the middle-class home. The inter-war period saw heightened levels of comfort in the children's library (although by no means everywhere, it should be emphasised). There was also an increase in the variety of decorative and spatial devices – from curtained windows and bright paintings, to inglenooks, work tables and raised performance platforms – which emphasised the role of the children's library as a place of relaxed free expression and constructive play.

Once economic recovery allowed the resumption of library construction from the late 1950s onwards, the post-Second World War era witnessed a proliferation of open-plan modernist designs, the roots of which can be traced back to earlier in the twentieth century, to the evolution and influence of Scandinavian design and to developments in the design of office space and European and American houses. In accordance with the universal spirit of modernism, adult and children's library's became more alike in their design: office-like – even space-age – efficiency replaced cosy domesticity.

Over the past generation, as increasing anxiety has been focused on the trajectory of the family in the fractured post-modern age and increasing importance has consequently been laid on nurturing and on early-years education, children's library design has in many ways reflected the cocooned 'comfort zone' of the domestic haven, itself the focus of a considerable commercialisation under the marketing influence of retail giants like IKEA and a vibrant culture of home improvement. In addition, as society experienced a marked strengthening of consumer and popular culture, the children's library took on the image of the playground, designs becoming more playful, vivid and hi-tech, the use of colour and the choice of furniture and fittings aping the McDonaldisation and Disneyisation of family-based mass leisure and entertainment.

Finally, taking an overview of the series of themes and periods we have identified, certain continuities and discontinuities present themselves. The early shelter function of the children's library can be seen today in its role as a cocooned 'comfort zone'. The original schoolroom image, though still visible in the 1920s and 1930s, and even detectable in the era of the children's library as 'modern office' in the 1960s, has now diminished. The open plan of post-war modernism was, naturally, in keeping with contemporary developments in office design, although it also reflected the emergence of the open-plan house, re-enacting the link of the children's library with the domestic sphere. Design for constructive play in the inter-war period has undergone a metamorphosis and has re-emerged in the early-twentieth century in the form of the children's library as playground. Heavy references to the domestic environment in the

1920s and 1930s have recently re-appeared under the guise of the high-styled IKEA-like environments for young library users; while, in keeping with the trend towards cocooning, the open-plan, free-flow interface with adult sections seems to have lost some of its appeal. But something that remains constant is the important place of the children's library and its design in public library provision, in Britain and elsewhere.

Children's Media Culture: A Key to Libraries of the Future?

Kirsten Drotner

DREAM: Danish Research Centre on Education and Advanced Media Materials

Media moves: convergence, commodification and globalisation

In many parts of the world, media are constitutive of children's everyday routines, their formation of social networks and their outlook on the world. For example, 40 per cent of Danish children aged 9-16 have media and ICTs as pretexts for meeting with their friends – the boys playing computer games, the girls often watching films together or listening to music; and these results resonate with trends in many European countries (Drotner, 2001: 164; Livingstone & Bovill, 2001, *Young People*, 2009). Watching television, playing computer games or exchanging personal updates on social networking sites such as FaceBook or Twitter are not additions to children's social lives, but are activities patterning the fabric of their everyday lives. Three related trends mark their uses, namely a technical convergence of all semiotic signs; economic commodification of products; and globalised processes of social participation.

We are currently witnessing a gradual merging of our television sets and radios, our print media, mobile phones and our computers and the internet. This convergence between media, telecommunication and ICTs is enabled by the technological possibilities of digitising all signs – text, sound, numbers, live and still images – and combining all of these signs on one platform. Some technologies are digital from their inception, such as the personal computer, games consoles and mobile devices; other technologies take on digital forms, such as digital television, e-books and radio podcasts. Over the last two decades, technological media convergence has been accompanied by financial convergence in the form of transborder mergers and acquisitions between large news corporations, internet providers, broadcasters and entertainment industries.

The complex constellation of current media are mostly developed by commercial enterprises and driven by logics of the market. While broadcast media such as radio and television share a past divided between commercial and public-service aims and often defined in relation to the nation state, computer gaming, online and mobile forms of communication are virtually all commercial products and services whose survival is largely dependent upon their success on globalised markets; and current clashes over ownership to online content (intellectual property rights versus creative commons) are clear demonstrations of the enormous financial investments made in media industries.

Taken together, convergence and commodification serve to blur existing boundaries between what is often named new and old media. Thus, ICTs, or new media, no longer develop in isolation from old media such as books, newspapers, radio or television. Moreover, the rapid domestication of these technologies in many parts of the world serve to shift people's interest from the new gadgets themselves onto their function, and this is particularly true of children. For example, they rarely want a new mobile phone because of a more advanced technology, but because they want to communicate in new ways, at different times and locales (Drotner, 2005; Ling, 2004).

In tandem with convergence, the last two decades have seen an intensified globalisation of media and ICT production, distribution, formats and applications. It is commonly agreed that today media are constitutive of cultural globalisation: the accelerated global flows of signs and cultural commodities by communication technologies serve to increase what John Tomlinson calls "complex connectivity" (Tomlinson, 1999: 2) – that is global, or transnational, media accentuate the interconnectedness of distinct cultures and modes of existence.

So far, a top-down perspective on globalisation has prevailed, a perspective that focuses upon the economic, technological, political and legal aspects of this complex connectivity. Studying children's uses of media, genres and formats that traverse geographical and temporal boundaries is one way of approaching media globalisation from a bottom-up perspective. Such a perspective of "mundane globalisation" (Drotner, 2004) may serve to substantiate and nuance the often very generalised top-down theories about cultural globalization, theories that also tend to be formulated as dichotomies between national and transnational (i.e. US) culture; between homogenisation and heterogenisation.

User trends: handling multimodalities, digital divides and otherness

The structural trends towards media digitisation, commodification and globalisation have important, and conflictual, implications for children's sociocultural existence and development. These implications are to do with shaping and sharing of multimodal resources; with cultures of participation and the formation of digital divides; and with handling semiotic and social forms of otherness.

Digital media facilitate children's cultural forms of production and exchange. Digitisation of all semiotic signs affords more seamless interweaving of text and numbers, images and sounds into multimodal mixtures that may be manipulated and easily exchanged. It should be noted that multimodality *per se* is not particular to digital media. Even the earliest books for children display a mixture of text and images, so the novelty of digital media is rather the ease with which different sign systems may be brought on to the same platform and manipulated there. Moreover, this manipulation of signs is also well-known from other media – writing letters or modifying photo negatives through special forms of development. Again, it is the relative ease with which such manipulations may be carried out that is particular to digital media – most children with access to a computer attempt to download music, images and text, and many edit and remix these signs in order to upload and share the results (Gilje 2008, Perkel 2008) – and this immediacy is unknown to analogue media apart from the telephone.

These processes involve often complex handlings of a range of semiotic codes and conventions. Several studies demonstrate that it takes a good deal of training to shape the complexity of semiotic resources in ways that are relevant not only to the young producers but also to the ones to which the results are addressed (Jewitt & Kress 2003, Tyner 1998). Very few children exert any form of digital literacy or multimodal literacy without systematic training.

Today, children's leisure cultures, not school, are the primary training grounds for what Henry Jenkins terms a "participatory culture" of digital media marked by online affiliations, creative expressions, collaborative problem-solving and mediated circulations (Jenkins et al. 2006). But, importantly, this culture operates on different forms of membership. Digital media are virtually all of a commercial nature, as we noted, and children's access to and appropriation of current media culture is unevenly distributed across divisions of region, class, gender and ethnicity. These so-called digital divides demonstrate an intimate connection to familiar fault lines in terms of class, gender, ethnicity, age and region (Fox 2005, Peter & Valkenburg 2006). Digital divides are often tackled by policy makers and educational stakeholders as problems of access, while their most drastic implications are possibly to do with inequalities of use – of children having very pronounced differences in terms of learning and knowing how to handle the complexities of media in ways that are relevant to their current lives and future livelihood (Warschauer 2004).

Divides in terms of cultural preferences and uses are a mainstay of modern childhood, and as such digital divides are no cause for analytical concern. But they should be cause for concern in terms of socio-cultural policies. This is because digital divides are increasingly being perceived as social divides. Widespread, global discourse that we live in information societies, knowledge societies, learning societies or network societies (Castells 1996, Hutchins 1968, Husén 1974, Ransom 1994, Stehr 1994) all point to the formative role played by the storage, formation, processing and increasingly mediatised communication of signs. A key competence is therefore semiotic competence, that is the ability to give shape to and handle multimodal expressions as part of everyday collaboration, communication and participation.

Children's mediatised leisure-time cultures offer important training grounds for the formation of multimodal semiotic resources. Uneven access to and appropriation of these resources therefore galvanise social inequalities to a degree not seen in previous generations whose life chances have been less dependent on semiotic competences. From this perspective, the choices made by public libraries in terms of their future resourcing of children attain a new dimension of relevance as we shall see below.

Irrespective of their actual options of engaging with different media and genres, children around the world know about their existence. This is because media globalisation both affords and enforces constant encounters with different representations of existence, different modes of communication and engagement, different ways of "being in the world". Children react to such mediatised forms of otherness with rejection, evasion, immersion or scepticism, but few are unaffected (Block & Buckingham 2007, Feilitzen & Carlsson 2002).

In empirical terms, then, there are no grounds for celebratory definitions of the rising generation through their unified media uses as is seen in both popular and academic discourses that variously term children a net generation (Tapscott, 1998), a digital generation (Papert, 1996), cyberkids (Holloway and Valentine, 2003) and the thumb tribes (Rheingold, 2002). Children are differently affected by current media trends and they react on these trends according to differences of age, gender, region and ethnicity. Yet, they all face a present and a future marked by their abilities to engage with and handle these increasingly digitised, commodified and globalised media. There are important questions, here, about how public libraries position themselves as resources for children in handling these complexities.

Changes in library output: new materials, new uses

The changing nature of children's media uses impacts on the ways in which public libraries operate in parts of the world marked by saturation of media access. For example, in Denmark the number of children visiting public libraries at least once a month has decreased from 51% in 1998 to 39% in 2004, while the number of children visiting less than once a month has risen from 28% in 1987 to 43% in 2004 (Bille et al., 2005: 183). Visits to school libraries have remained at a stable high percentage: 91% of Danish children visit at least once a month against 93% in 1998 (Bille et al., 2005: 182), perhaps because school libraries operate as resources for explicit learning processes rather than as individual leisure-time options as is the case for public libraries.

Developed on a notion of cultural scarcity of access, many public libraries still focus on facilitating children's physical access to print materials. Naturally, this focus is vital as a prerequisite of use in parts of the world where cultural scarcity is an issue, and to groups of users for whom access is difficult. In Denmark, as in many other countries, libraries vie for children's attention in competition with other cultural arenas; and so here the challenge is not so much to offer access as to offer diversity of good quality materials and diversity of uses.

Public libraries need to widen their output of materials to include all modes of representation – print, sound, still and moving images – and, in fact, this has been a requirement of public libraries in Denmark since 2000. Today, Danish children make less use of the library for book loans while they demonstrate a keen interest in borrowing film and music, just as online gaming is a popular pastime in the physical library, particularly for boys aged 10-13 (Drotner, Jørgensen & Nyboe 2006). Children diversify their library uses into physical and virtual uses in a process of transformation that has been termed the hybrid library (Thorhauge, 2001), the performative library (Graulund, 2006) and the library as a third space between private and public places (Oldenburg, 1999).

Public libraries are still key catalysts for children's freedom of expression. But their role is shifting from safeguarding access to information and entertainment on to facilitating young users' transformation of abundant and often chaotic bits of information into coherent knowledge that facilitate their sensemaking processes. In terms of entertainment, a major challenge is to offer what children would not easily encounter in visits to the local mall or surfing the internet. Very importantly, connections made across various modes of expression are hard for children to acquire, for example in recognition of genre similaries or thematic parallels. Since such connections help animate young users' sense of aesthetic quality and contextual awareness, they are important aspects in fulfilling the aims set in the UN Convention of securing cultural quality and diversity.

Related to the increased importance played by appropriations rather than access is the diversification of quality control. Library professionals are no longer gatekeepers of cultural quality through their choice of materials offered in the physical library. Children can, and do, order materials online, they snap up bits of information and interesting stories from a range of sources; and so the mere presence of materials in the physical library is little guide in children's cultural choices. The changing nature of cultural access and quality control both enforce and allow new relations to be forged between young users and library professionals.

Changes in input: New professional skills

Like most other public-service institutions, libraries have based their modes of communication with the public on what may be termed a sender perspective, i.e. a perspective focusing on institutional priorities of dissemination. Faced by increasing competition not least from commercial providers of cultural output, many public libraries have sought to attune themselves more to a user perspective, sensitising themselves to different user groups and their immediate cultural preferences. While this shift of perspective has operated as an important eye-opener for many libraries in terms of priorities of leadership and more contextual understanding of users, it has also implied a more consumer-oriented view on users, in the sense that users tend to be defined through their concrete choice of materials.

If public libraries are to remain resources for children's freedom of expression under the changed conditions outlined above, one of their major challenges is to develop more holistic strategies of communication with users. Such strategies must be sensitive to children's everyday lives and their diversified contexts of cultural appropriation; they must demonstrate abilities of quality assessment across a range of cultural expressions; and they must be able to juggle the different demands of the virtual and physical libraries.

Realising such strategies is no small feat. There are important questions to be asked about professional education of the future, of changing demands made on physical library places, and last, but not least, of professional communication skills. In a Danish context, a recent white paper on the future of libraries for children outlines some answers to these questions based on in-depth analysis of children's cultures in general and their library uses in particular (Brandt & Poulsen 2008). By way of conclusion, I would like to comment on the changing demands made on professional communication skills. This aspect is perhaps of particular relevance in communicating with children brought up with demands on individual distinction and attainment. A dialogical approach has proved to work well under these circumstances, an approach that balances respect for age and gender differences with an insistence on professional insights and expertise (Drotner, Jørgensen & Nyboe 2006). Key catalysts for the formation of such a dialogic approach are joint spaces of professional reflection, i.e. joint reflections "on practice in practice" conducted in close proximity to institutional routines, yet with room for ruptures of these routines through a shifting of perspective.

Culture as societal lever

The issues raised in this article touch on basic rationales for the future development of libraries as forms of public service resourcing the public good. Following the arguments outlined above means redrawing conventional boundaries of understanding for library services that are in a process of transformation from established definitions as archives of books and other print media. Naturally, such transformations must respect divergences of users, materials, professional organisations and legal frameworks. Still, it may be in order to hold on to the common policy rationales that also underlie the needs for transformation. For example, the European Union a few years ago defined culture as a key lever of citizenship, community building and civic engagement (European Commission 2007). In a situation in which most other cultural resources are defined and developed as commodities on competing markets, it seems vital to retain such a perspective in order to facilitate the promotion of cultural diversity for the young library users who are citizens of tomorrow. Public libraries are fundamental cultural resources for civic societies, and they may draw on strong traditions in serving their local communities. Hence contemporary librarians across all domains of service occupy an opportune position to realise visions of the future for the future.

References

Block, Liesbeth de & David Buckingham (eds) (2007) *Global Children, Global Media: Migration, Media and Childhood* Basingstoke: Palgrave.

Brandt, Anna Enemark & Ann Poulsen (eds) Fremtidens biblioteksbetjening af børn [Children's future library service] Copenhagen: Danish Library Association. Retrieved September 2011 from: www.bs.dk/publikationer/andre/fremtidens/index.htm

Castells, Manuel (1996) *The rise of the network society. Vol. 1: The Information age: Economy, society and culture* Oxford: Blackwell.

Convention on the Rights of the Child (1989). United Nations. Retrieved September 2011 from: http://www2.ohchr.org/english/law/crc.htm

Drotner, Kirsten, Heidi Jørgensen & Lotte Nyboe (2006) *Børnebiblioteket som læringsrum: kultur, kommunikation og transformation* [The children's library as space for learning: culture, communication, transformation] Aarhus: Aarhus Public Libraries. Retrieved September 2011 from: http://www.bibliotekogmedier.dk/fileadmin/user_upload/doku menter/bibliotek/indsatsomraader/boern/Bibliotekstilbud_til_boern/Litteratur_og_links/ Boernebiblioteket_som_laeringsrum.pdf

Drotner, Kirsten (2005) Media on the Move: Personalised Media and the Transformation of Publicness, pp. 187-211 in Sonia Livingstone (ed.) *Audiences and Publics: When Cultural Engagement Matters for the Public Sphere* Bristol: Intellect Books.

Drotner, Kirsten (2001) *Medier for fremtiden: børn, unge og det nye medielandskab* [Media For the Future: Children, Young People and the Changing Media Environment] Copenhagen: Høst og Søn.

Drotner, Kirsten (2004) Disney Discourses, or Mundane Globalisation, pp. 91-115 in Ib Bondebjerg & Peter Golding (eds) *European Culture and the Media* Bristol: Intellect Books.

European Commission. (2007). *Communication from the Commission to the European Parliament, the Council, the European Economic and Social Committee and the Committee of the Regions on a European agenda for culture in a globalizing world*. Retrieved September 2011 from: http://eur-lex.europa.eu/LexUriServ/LexUriServ.do?uri=COM:2007:0242:FIN:EN:PDF.

Feilitzen, Cecilia von & Ulla Carlsson (eds) (2002) *Children, Young People and Media Globalization* Gothenburg: Nordicom.

Fox, Susannah (2005) *Digital Divisions: The Pew Internet and American Life Project*. Retrieved September 2011 from: http://www.pewinternet.org

Gilje, Øystein (2008) Googling Movies: Digital Media Production and the "Culture of Appropriation", pp. 29-48 in Kirsten Drotner, Hans Siggaard-Jensen & Kim Christian Schrøder (eds) *Informal Learning and Digital Media: Constructions, Contexts, Critique* Cambridge: Cambridge Scholars Publishing.

Graulund, Jan (2006) Folkebiblioteket: et rum for dannelse [The public library: room for character formation], pp. 55-71 in: L. Emerek et al. *Folkebiblioteket som forvandlingsrum: perspektiver på folkebiblioteket i kultur- og medielandskabet [The public library as a space of transformation: perspectives on the public library in the landscape of culture and media]* Copenhagen: Danish Library Association.

Holloway, Sarah L. & Gill Valentine (2003) *Cyberkids: Children in the Information Age* London: RoutledgeFalmer.

Husén, Torsten (1974) *The learning society* London: Methuen.

Hutchins, R. M. (1968) *The learning society* Harmondsworth: Penguin.

Jenkins, Henry, Katie Clinton, Ravi Purushotma, Alice J. Robinson, & Margaret Weigel, (2006) *Confronting the Challenges of Participatory Culture: Media Education for the 21st Century.* Building the field of digital media and learning. The John D. and Catherine T. MacArthur Foundation. Retrieved September 2011 from: http://digitallearning.macfound.org/atf/cf/%7B7E45C7E0-A3E0-4B89-AC9C-E807E1B0AE4E%7D/JENKINS_WHITE_PAPER.PDF

Ling, Richard (2004) *The Mobile Connection: The Cell Phone's Impact on Society* San Fransisco: Morgan Kaufmann.

Livingstone, Sonia & Moira Bovill (eds) (2001) *Children and their Changing Media Environment: A European Comparative Study* Mahwah, NJ: Lawrence Erlbaum Associates.

Oldenburg, R. (1999) *The great good place: Cafés, coffee shops, bookstores, bars, hair salons and other hangouts at the heart of a community*. New York: Marlowe.

Papert, Seymour (1996) *The Connected Family: Bridging the Digital Generation Gap* Longstreet Press.

Perkel, Dan (2008) Copy and Paste Literacy? Literacy Practices in the Production of a MySpace Profile, pp. 203-24 in Kirsten Drotner, Hans Siggaard-Jensen & Kim Christian Schrøder (eds) *Informal Learning and Digital Media: Constructions, Contexts, Critique* Cambridge: Cambridge Scholars Publishing.

Peter, Jochen, & Patti M. Valkenburg (2006) Adolescents' Internet Use: Testing the 'Disappearing Digital Divide' versus the 'Emerging Differentiation' Approach, *Poetics,* vol. 34, no. 4-5: 293-305.

Ransom, S. (1994) *Towards the learning society* London: Cassell.

Rheingold, Howard (2002) *Smart Mobs: The New Social Revolution* Cambridge, MA: Perseus Publishing.

Stehr, N. 1994. *Knowledge societies* London: Sage.

Tapscott, Don (1998) *Growing Up Digital: The Rise of the Net Generation.* New York: McGraw-Hill.

Thorhauge, Jens (2001) Børnekulturen i udvikling: biblioteket og de andre institutioner i opbrud [Development of children's culture: the transformation of the library and other institutions]. In: A. Bülow & M. Hassel (eds), *Børnekulturen i grænselandet mellem amter og kommuner [Children's Culture across the boundaries of counties and city councils]* Copenhagen: Children's Cultural Council.

Tomlinson, John (1999) *Globalization and Culture* Cambridge: Polity Press.

Tyner, Kathleen (1998) *Literacy in a Digital World* Mahwah, NJ: Lawrence Erlbaum Associates.

Warschauer, Mark (2004) *Technology and Social Inclusion: Rethinking the Digital Divide,* Cambridge, MA: MIT Press.

Young People in the European Digital Media Landscape: A Statistical Overview with an Introduction by Sonia Livingstone and Leslie Haddon (2009) Gothenburg: NORDICOM.

A Children's Public Library in Muscat, Oman

James R. Keller
VITETTA Library Design Studio, Philadelphia, USA

In the summer of 2007 approximately forty interested citizens developed the concept of the first Public Library for Children and Families in Oman. The founders formed a Board of Directors to realize their vision – with Her Highness Seyyida, Dr. Mona Al Said as the Honorary Chair and Dr. Samira Moosa as Board Chair.

The Board created a Vision Statement in the autumn of 2007 and selected our firm – VITETTA of Philadelphia – to prepare a feasibility study and the subsequent architectural design.

Children's Public Library in Muscat, Oman   Architects: VITETTA / COWI

Figure 1. Oman © Croese, Jaap. 2006 "Oman – A Pictorial Tour", Motivate Publishing: 55

In January, 2008 the Board received the gift of the building site from His Highness Seyyid Haitham, Minister of Heritage and Culture, as well as financial support from the private sector – in particular funding for design from the Oman Oil Company, Mr. Ahmed Al Wahabi, C.E.O.

The building is now funded and, in September 2011, about to begin construction pending some revisions of the local code on the part of the Muscat Municipality.

The site for the Children's Public Library is located west of the Muttrah – the city market in Muscat – Oman's capital city. The site is relatively flat and narrow – stretching east to west. To the north is an ocean inlet and surrounding marsh that is rich with biodiversity.

Figure 2. Site of Children's Public Library, Muscat

As part of the planning, a focus group was conducted with twenty two boys and girls from Muscat. The children represented a cross section of socio-economic backgrounds and included several children from the local orphanage.

A recent survey indicates there are over 190,000 children between 6 months and 19 years of age in Muscat alone. Therefore, part of the Founders vision is that; "The Library is to provide free access to library resources and services – to the children of Oman from birth to 18 years of age."

Children's Public Library in Muscat, Oman   Architects: VITETTA/COWI

Figure 3. Children's play area © Dr Samira Moos

The Library will be a destination for children and families of Oman, and will be a model for sustainable design and progressive library service concepts for the region. The architecture will embody the spirit, history and beauty of Omani architecture and yet will incorporate progressive elements that will define its character.

Figure 4. Model of Children's Library, Muscat © Dutch Huff, VITTETTE – Model by TAG
    Architectural Models

The Library will evoke its mission of literacy, learning and community
through its materials, scale, spatial rhythm and the use of colour.

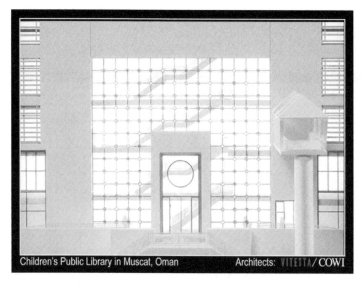

Figure 5. Model of Children's Library, Muscat © Dutch Huff,
          VITTETTE – Model by TAG Architectural Models

Service to children will be celebrated through the use of imaginative interior spaces and light. Coloured glass, tactile materials, textures of surfaces and other timeless architectural elements will be used in synthesis to create mystery, discovery, comfort and delight.

Figure 6. Interior spaces, Children's Public Library, Muscat © Dutch Huff,
          VITTETTE – Model by TAG Architectural Models

The Library will be a complement to the neighbouring Children's Museum, Museum of Natural History and future Children's Theatre. The Library will connect with these buildings by means of learning gardens and pathways.

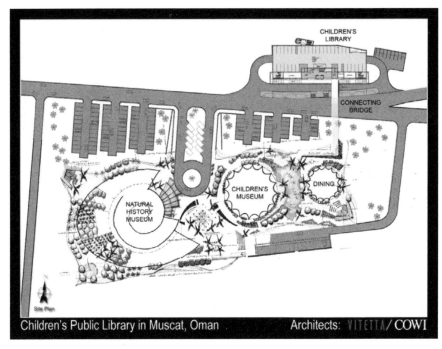

Figure 7. Landscape plan for Children's Library, Muscat © VITETTE/Matt Arnn, Landscape Architect, US Forestry NE Division

The Library will connect with its beautiful natural surroundings by orienting views and maximizing natural connections to the environment.

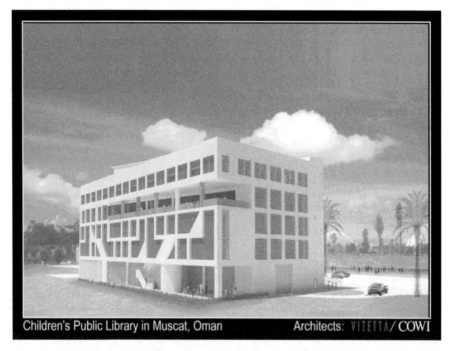

Figure 8. Children's Public Library, Muscat maximising natural connections to the environment.

The arrival at the Library will be an important part of the sequence of travel to, through, and from the building. The sequence of movement throughout the building will be clear and inviting.

Children's Public Library in Muscat, Oman   Architects: VITETTA/ COWI

Figure 9. Entrance to Children's Public Library, Muscat

The Library will be entered from the raised street level centre entrance through the Lobby. The Atrium Lobby will feature coloured glass discs that will cast prisms of colour throughout the space by day and will glow from outside by night.

Children's Public Library in Muscat, Oman   Architects: VITETTA/ COWI

Figure 10. Model of the atrium lobby, Children's Library, Muscat © Dutch Huff, VITTETTE – Model by TAG Architectural Models

The design will maximize the use of architectural form, scale and materials in unusual ways to create interest and even drama. The second level of the library sets back from the north wall to provide dramatic views up and through the space from the first level. A zig zag formed cantilever informs and invites the first level customers – young and elementary school age children – that something exciting awaits above – the second level – where the teen and young adult space is found.

Children's Public Library in Muscat, Oman   Architects: VITETTA/ COWI

Figure 11. Second level

The first level of the library will contain the early childhood and parenting area to the west (or left of the plan) and the elementary age area to the east (or right). Features of this floor are the Omani seating area – an area with cushions on the floor to create a traditional conversation area – and an area called "Visions to the World". The "Visions to the World" area will have interactive display, computers and collections of world geography/culture and arts. This level is not only open to view the floor above at the north side, but also to expansive views of the sea.

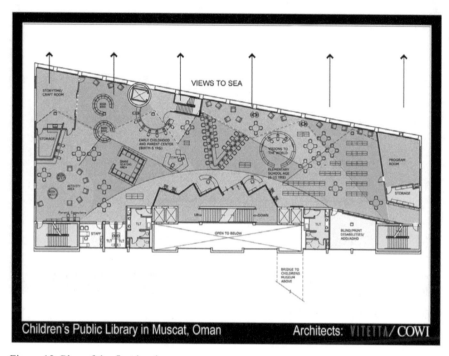

Figure 12. Plan of the first level

The second level will contain the young teen area to the west (or left of the plan) and the young adult area to the east (or right). This level will also contain the administrative offices and a special collection area for persons with visual disabilities. This level overlooks level one through the cut out at the zig zag glass wall – sharing vistas to the park and sea.

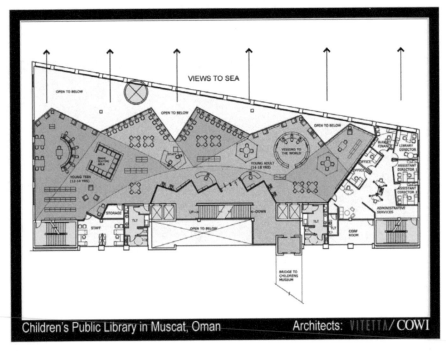

Figure 13. Plan of the second level

The third level will contain a large meeting room, small meeting/conference room, a computer training lab, staff workroom and hall gallery. The fourth floor (not shown) is an open floor for tenant rental and income for the Library.

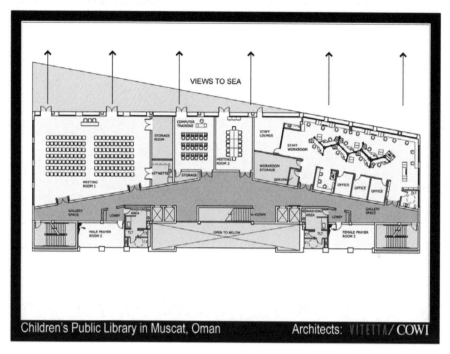

Children's Public Library in Muscat, Oman   Architects: VITETTA / COWI

Figure 14. Plan of the third level

Sustainable design elements include a green roof terrace for special pro-grammes.

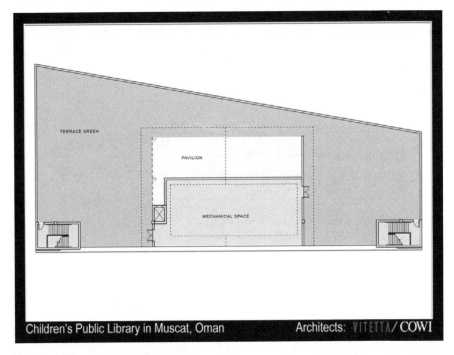

Figure 15. Plan of green roof terrace

The optimal direction for ambient light in Muscat is north, where large un-shaded windows will provide abundant light and breath-taking views of the coastline. The colouration of the window openings will provide a playful inter-action of shape, form, void and colour both by day and by night.

Figure 16. Windows providing light and views of the coastline © Dutch Huff, VITTETTE – Model by TAG Architectural Models

The Library will be a building that children and families will want to visit, both for its programmes, collections and services, and also for its sense of place. The Library will inspire children of all ages to learn, grow, and be a part of the community – both in Oman and globally.

Figure 17.   Model of Children's Public Library, Muscat © Dutch Huff,
VITTETTE – Model by TAG Architectural Models

The Library will be a place of calm and a place of activity, a place that inspires creativity and stirs the imagination.

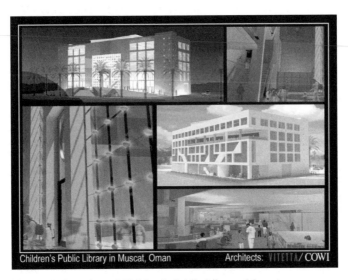

Figure 18. Overview of Children's Public Library, Muscat

Building Excellent Libraries with and for Children

Inci Önal

Department of Information Management
Faculty of Letters, Hacettepe University

Introduction

Educational and humanitarian ideals aside, service to children is a fantastic investment for the library. While adult library services respond mainly to people who come into the library, school and children's librarians often reach out into the community. Library directors applaud and support librarians who will bring a new generation of children into the library. Children's librarians have always been expected to reach out and develop relationships with children who use school and children's libraries (Anderson 1987). Most public, school and children's libraries offer core services for children. In order to create a workable programme of services to be offered, collaboration with children will be very important.

A number of factors contribute to an excellent library service – buildings, services, different collections, organizational structures, classification systems, awareness of users' needs, sufficient budgets, technological developments and cultural practices. Building new libraries with and for children will provide evidence that a new approach to library construction will result in higher use. The broad-based findings are supported by research articles describing children's libraries as popular, active, and busy facilities. The fact is that we know very little about what children think of how to plan an excellent programme of library services or how children would design school and children's libraries if they were the library director. In this research, children described many aspects of libraries. By indicating which managerial, physical and design characteristics they feel lead to high quality children and/or school libraries, children are indirectly indicating what they believe the function of these libraries should be.

Libraries Built for Children

Designing libraries for children is a complex task. The planner and designer must have a thorough knowledge of what children's librarianship is and how children's libraries function. They must be aware that library services are planned for children's use in school and children's libraries and are viewed and valued as educational, scientific, social, cultural, entertainment and information centres even if good use is not always made of them by the very children for whom they are designed.

Children's librarianship—a term that encompasses all library services to children (aged zero to eighteen) in school and public library settings—has long been considered important as cultural and educational services in the community. Designing a children's or school library involves the proper planning and design of built environments to accommodate the social, physical, psychological, and behavioural needs of people (Jenkins 2000). The reality of designing libraries is that there are many groups involved, including librarians, architects, interior designers, administrators, consultants and , of course, users – in this case children.

New developments in web–based technologies in society at large offer opportunities for more dynamic models in libraries. Advancements in educational technologies have served to encourage or inhibit four characteristics in library services design: interactivity, scalability, media-richness, and granularity. Information technologies and Internet-based computing, the current hallmark of twenty-first century library services, offer the technical capacity to address all four characteristics.

Children's Participation in Excellent Library Design

Children's participation in library design provides some potential benefits and focuses on the children's specific efforts acting as directors in creating the sort of environment they want in a school and/or children's library. Children's participation acts as an opportunity to rehearse experiences, uses their intense developmental need for social experiences with peers, offers opportunities to employ their fledgling hypothetical thinking abilities, and channels their enormous emotional and physical energies. It gives children not only the opportunity to use their energies in constructive ways but also a different perspective on what it means to be part of a community – whether that community be their school, or their public library (Boone 2002; Campbell and Shlechter 1979; Miller 2002). In addition to the enormous benefits for the children involved, creating a dynamic programme through children's participation is beneficial to the library and the librarian.

For users, especially children or students, to contribute to the development of better libraries, it is important to understand how library facilities affect students and other occupants. It is also important that plans and programmes address the needs of users. Architects and library committee members can study the effects of a specific type of building technology, analyze furniture plans, develop plans for moving, and so on, while children could investigate how they, as library directors, might modify their libraries to ensure designs meet their real needs.

Review of Related Literature

There is a wealth of information on child participation and group decision making to be found in the literature of a variety of disciplines. Theoretical foundations have been borrowed from the fields of planning, librarianship, management, architecture, and communications because the phenomena of child participation is so complex (Banduric 1993; Cooper and Matthews 2000; Edwards 1990; Foote 2004; Goulding 2009; IFLA 2003; Koontz 2007; Rohlf 1986; Sannwald 1997; Sannwald 2007) and can be summarized as follows:

- to have a good library building is a major determinant of use;
- recent articles by architects and librarians, written a decade apart, show a shift in thinking about libraries from collection-focused to user-focused facilities;
- the library as a learning space has to be flexible, compact, accessible, extendible, varied, organized, comfortable, functional, ergonomic, electronically equipped, colour sensitive, controlled, secure and economical;
- despite the provision of satisfactory library facilities, children's library use may fall dramatically if children lack motivation to use library;
- library building has the potential to support community engagement, leading to a new era of library-based activity;
- library design standards dictate that libraries be easily accessible to children who must form the lifelong reading habit;
- programmes designed to maximize use of the library meet growing population needs with higher budget and staff allocations;
- the primary design participants are the librarians directly responsible for the library;
- a common mistake in the physical design of a library is planning buildings for the professionals and not for the users;
- individuals with formal design training, as well as individuals without design training, have responsibility for the library environment, and users may contribute to the design of the libraries;
- participants are allowed to identify potential solutions;
- checklists are utilized by many librarians as primary guidelines for library building programmes, and are considered useful;
- librarians are constantly faced with changing conditions, values, suggestions, and interrelationships. The most important thing is the ability to learn from past mistakes and to change methods in the future.

The use of participants, especially children' participation, in planning, building and design processes is highly touted by many librarians, planners, and designers. Most of the literature in building libraries and architecture indicates an endorsement of the process.

Characteristics of an Excellent Library

Technological advances have resulted in better accessibility of documents and have improved the service to children. Making predictions about the characteristics of an excellent library has become a popular pursuit. It has included many predictions, recommendations and expectations for developing facilities, systems and technology to improve the quality of existing structures, as well as the creation of both aesthetically pleasing library buildings and efficiently organized services. In planning new facilities, realistic predictions of both current and future needs can be made. After determining the needs, the planning committee should explore ways that these needs might be met. Children, too, can be drawn into the planning process by being asked for suggestions about, or for pictures of, their vision of the new library.

The characteristics of excellent libraries that affect the library service to children include: utilization of knowledge, social need, library operations, use of technology, library policies and procedures, a productive work environment, staff and budget policies, intellectual freedom and censorship, community public relations, organizing special events, building libraries and planning facilities and, indeed, concepts of library and information science. All of the characteristics noted have had an effect on how children's and school libraries are organized and how they work. The building, planning and design of library facilities have been emphasized throughout this research.

Research Design and Methods

In spite of numerous publications on library buildings, research on children's participation in the planning and design of library facilities has been minimal. Without research, librarians can rely only on common beliefs and their own personal experiences to make planning and management decisions. We do not know how current children's library services compare with school libraries in Turkey, what the key factors are, why children are using the libraries, which design criteria for good libraries are important from a child's viewpoint, and what the recommendations for the future would be if the child were director. Without this knowledge librarians cannot be sure that spaces are being designed as children would want, whether the spaces meet the needs and expectations of the children who use them, or if the services in these libraries relate to the mission of their institution. The purpose of this study is to explore children's awareness, interest, and actual practice in relation to library design and children's / school library services. This study is designed to answer the following research questions:

- How do children's library services compare with the school libraries in Turkey? What are the key factors in planning new children's / school library buildings?
- Why are children using these libraries?
- Which design criteria for excellent libraries are important from the children's point of view?
- What would be the recommendations for future designs if the child were to be the director?

The survey research method was designed to answer these research questions. The initial plan was to interview library staff and school administrators about services and facilities for children. The researcher, however, decided to interview the children themselves. Adana, Ankara, Bayburt, Corum, Diyarbakir, Edirne, Erzurum, Gaziantep, Istanbul, Izmir, Kahramanmaras, Manisa, Mersin, Samsun, and Tunceli, in Turkey were selected randomly. A total of 51 libraries (14 public library children's departments, 5 children's libraries, 32 school libraries) were identified to form the study population. 458 children aged between 7–11 years in the different schools in Turkey were asked to make paintings based on the use and design of children's and/or school libraries. Asking children what they think and paint recognises that they are well able to speak for themselves and have unrivalled insights into their own feelings and needs. This study is different from most others in this field because it acquires data both from children who use school libraries (315 students) and children who use children's libraries (143 children) in their role as putative designers and library directors and therefore is relevant to both of these library types. This study was exploratory, descriptive, and evaluative in nature. It focuses on research with children rather than research about children.

Building Excellent Libraries with and for Children

1. Survey Results: Library Services for Children

There are a number of important factors to consider when designing children's library services or planning school library programmes in Turkey. A summary of these factors is provided in Table 1.

Table 1 shows the potential of integrating learning, knowledge and service components. We know that there were often strong connections between children's libraries and school libraries. Innovative formats produced by technological and societal influences have been expected in children's programming and services for a long time. To redesign processes and examine space requirements in an organization for children services, it is necessary to analyze the existing situation carefully and to identify integration potentials (Önal 1995; Önal 2005; Önal 2006; Önal 2009). This paper generally focuses on the ongoing traditional children's library services in both public and school libraries in Turkey.

Components	Children's Libraries	School Libraries
History	During the period of the Ottoman Empire, these were founded by sultans, statesmen and wealthy people by private endowments, which were charitable pious foundations called "waqfs"; beautiful cabinets for books and a separate room for children	Goes back to the 1700s in elementary, secondary and higher levels (mosque schools, madrasa, enderun); decorated in an artistic style
Establishment	Influenced by the reforms in the field of education and culture since 1925; requirements for Public and Children's Libraries Bylaw since 1981	Influenced by the reforms in the field of education and culture since 1857; requirements for School Libraries Bylaw since 1959
Governance	Administered by the General Directorate of the Ministry of Culture and Tourism; contact with public library service centres	The Ministry of National Education; administration units are separated but has horizontal and vertical connections with each other
Number of libraries	1096 public libraries with children's department; 46 separate children's libraries	57 837 school libraries of various types and at various levels of education
Aims	To provide user – centred services	To develop quality programmes and services
Building	A standard project is applied; very dull coloured decoration; not functional	Some kind of space or room for the library in all schools; no special facilities
Furniture plans	Ergonomic requirements for furnishings	Requirements for designing successful furniture plans
Finance	Financed by the General Directorate of the Ministry of Culture and Tourism;	Financed by the Ministry of National Education; sponsorship from private organisations;

Components	Children's Libraries	School Libraries
	sponsorship from private organisations	donations by national and/or international organisations
Staff	Librarians, administrative staff, voluntary helpers	Librarians, teachers and non-professional staff
Collection	Basic collection on children's literature	Basic research and recreation
Types of media	Print formats, audiovisual materials, electronic resources and environments	Print formats, audiovisual materials, electronic resources and environments
Users	In 2010, some 76 million people live in Turkey, the number of children is approximately 30 million. Can charge membership fee	In 2010, some 76 million people live in Turkey, the number of students was approximately 20 million. Serves whole school free of charge
Services	Information services; audio-visual services; storytelling; reading for pleasure; media presentations in special programmes	Curriculum based information services; homework assistance; creative activities; information literacy teaching units; reading development programmes
Cooperation	Cooperation between the public library and media centre; contact with local public libraries and branch libraries	Sharing of resources between different organizations common feature

Table 1. Comparative table: Children's and school library systems in Turkey

2. Survey Results: Moving into New Facilities

Every school has a school library and every public library also has children's library services in Turkey. This emphasized that the strengths are services, resources, location and equipment. Turkish school and children's library services are near the users (Önal 2009; Önal 2006; Turkiye Cumhuriyeti Kültür Bakanlığı 1981; Turkiye Cumhuriyeti Maarif Vekaleti 1959; Turkiye Cumhuriyeti Milli Egitim Bakanligi 1976; Turkiye…2001; Turkiye…2006; Turkiye… 2009).

We can implement better children's services with their, the children's, help. This study attempts to identify and describe ideal learning environments by drawing on children's new and existing experiences to provide design guidance.

72 Inci Önal

Table 2 provides very interesting results about children's experiments and suggestions for managing children's services. The children's propositions provide a starting point for thinking about potential future issues in library design in school and children's libraries. The design and physical arrangement for the library must accommodate a diverse range of services as suggested by the children (see Table 2).

Evaluation Areas	Children's Library Users %	School Library Users %
Library Use		
– Very helpful	27	19
– Sometimes helpful	43	38
– Rarely helpful	22	32
– Non use	8	11
Most Important Library Services*		
– Connecting people to information		
– Computers and Internet access	71	88
– Collection of materials	68	80
– Physical place	65	77
– Social and cultural activities	47	78
– Reference assistance	35	67
– Services and resources for children	36	55
– Other		
	33	51
	25	48
Total (N)	**100** **(N=315)**	**100** **(N=143)**

Table 2. Percentage of children's responses for library use and important library services (*The items list the responses that were mentioned more than once)

3. Survey Results: Identifying New Libraries

An ideal library design is an effective combination of many related functions.

The library building deriving from children's views incorporated a wide range of choices and services, and accommodated many different needs. These included:

3.1 – Library building: libraries and their environments are designed for a large number of social, cultural, and learning activities. They have always supported learning, satisfaction, happiness, and effectiveness. The most effective location for children's services is at the heart of the school and public libraries.

3.2 – Study areas: the library has an intimate and welcoming atmosphere both inside and outside with mobile shelves, chairs and tables.

3.3 – A centralized reference desk staffed to monitor and service all key areas: the reference desk should represent the many functions that take place in the library, such as research, computers, browsing, community activities, self–education and children's services.

3.4 – 24 hour study areas: these areas include comfortable, easily supervised, and adequately heated, cooled, and lighted study areas for long–term use. Traditional quiet places to learn and study are also important. Computers and books are distributed throughout the library – at the entrance, in the book stacks, near reading places, and at user service points.

3.5 – Virtual space without walls: ergonomically-designed electronic work-stations, stand up E-panels in the stacks, embedded terminals, wireless mobile laptop stations, and a variety of computer configurations.

3.6 – Soft seating areas: a tea/juice/milk service area for casual meetings and book discussions; physical space with many different types of spaces for lots of different purposes are open during library hours.

3.7 – Multiuse, unfurnished areas: open space is vital to the proper functioning of a facility but it is necessary to avoid designing anything that encourages young children to run, jump, or climb. The planning of furniture includes form, shape and colour, in relation to use, as well as durability and flexibility.

3.8 – 21ˢᵗcentury library design: comfortable places, meeting and study rooms, teen- friendly areas, technology points, wall hangings, Atatürk posters, bestsellers, DVDs, downloadable audio books, answers to life issues, and original environments are welcomed.

Children identified which criteria for excellence in library design are important in their view. As Table 3 clearly shows, these criteria and functions are more general than the aforementioned services and physical characteristics; children's painting and listing responses were mentioned more than once.

Evaluation Areas	Children's Library Users %	School Library Users %
Design Criteria for Excellent Libraries *		
— Central library building	71	83
— Welcoming study areas	66	74
— Access to information for children	65	70
— 24 hour study areas	44	62
— Virtual space that removes the walls	38	57
— Soft seating areas	31	55
— Multiuse, unfurnished areas	28	42
— 21st century library design	26	30
Total (N)	**100** **(N=315)**	**100** **(N=143)**

Table 3. Design Criteria for Excellence Library
(*The items list the responses that were mentioned more than once)

4. Survey Results: If I were Director...

From a designer's point of view, getting the views of children and students in the role of director, is of interest but the views can be somewhat unrealistic because design features that may work in the early phases of a library service lifecycle may turn out as optimistic in the later phases. The views identified were:

4.1 – Being a director: children are interested in being a director and providing attractive library environments for other children.

4.2 – Building a library: designing a library affects behaviour. Building libraries and designing spaces can support satisfaction, happiness, and effectiveness.

To create programmes designed to maximize the use of the library, children need librarians who will focus services on new populations – children. Asked to describe the sort of libraries they would design if they were the director, children identified many traits and skills as useful and necessary for today's and tomorrow's librarians. See the summary of these responses below in Table 4.

Evaluation Areas	Children's Library Users %	School Library Users %
Ideal Library Director Traits and Characteristics*		
– Beautiful or handsome, gentle, patient, smiling	93	91
– Selecting materials	76	84
– Wants to work with all children	65	77
– Designing spaces	66	72
– Teaching computers and Internet access	33	67
– Bringing about change	25	61
– Services and resources for children	23	55
– Reading fairly tales to children	21	47
– Others	19	37
Total (N)	**100** (N=315)	**100** (N=143)

Table 4. Percentage of children's planned actions if they were directors
(*The items list the responses that were mentioned more than once)

Findings

Children's participation has been used as a strategy in planning, building, design and management. If children were directors and participating in a real–life planning and design project, they could develop a sense of societal responsibility and learn what it is to be genuinely involved. This research has been designed to get a general picture of children's experiences or thoughts and the factors influencing them. In expressing themselves using their own concepts and vocabularies, the children described their ideal library. In order to meet current expectations, children's views will no longer be an isolated activity (see Table 5).

1. Nature of Library Building and Designing	2. Expectations for Excellence in Library Building and Designing
Individual planning	Cooperative planning
Small libraries	The new library building is larger than the old
Public access computers	The growing importance of electronics, wireless network coverage, high tech devices for learning and playing, digital media centres
Libraries to share space with non-library functions	The new library space for library purposes

1. Nature of Library Building and Designing	2. Expectations for Excellence in Library Building and Designing
Minimum windows	Lots of windows, lighting, ventilation, multi-level facilities, heating, climate control, planned decor, restrooms, indoor air quality
Special places to read, rooms arranged for traffic flow	The number of group and collaborative study rooms, quiet places, places where noise and conversation would be allowed, traffic flow, staff–only areas, exhibition spaces, play areas, rooms for arts and crafts
Decorative areas	Bright colours, both primary and fluorescent, wall hangings and posters of cartoon characters, child-related bulletin boards, exhibition cases, beautiful and well designed areas
Traditional shelves and study rooms	Compact shelving, open stacks, and automatic storage retrieval systems, safety and security
General-use seating	More comfortable, accessible, plentiful, flexible, and soft library seating typically described as lounges, couches, places for social interaction and other types of non-task specific chairs (e.g., computer table chairs)

Table 5. Nature of library building and expectations for excellence in library building as exemplified in children's and school library systems

On the one hand, these research results indicate the basic profile of libraries. On the other hand, they indicate not only current library services but also expected future services. Children identified library and non-library facilities in new buildings ranging from soft seating areas to children's meeting rooms. Increasingly, the children want to use libraries as places for social, educational and cultural events. Libraries also continue to expand and enhance user space by including more table seating as well as playing areas, often far more than in existing facilities, especially in children's and school libraries. We hope that new libraries with multiuse spaces will be increasingly designed to be places where children's activities play a central role.

From a methodological point of view, what we urgently need are design guidelines grounded in empirical research, in particular research that looks into the development of user expectations over longer periods of time. It is hoped that by putting children's suggestions into practice, libraries will be able to develop their services with children's experiences in mind and to cope with today's changing world. Children's and school librarians should be encouraged to be involved in design and service planning as often as possible.

Conclusion

A children's and/or school library is a visible symbol of a community's commitment to provide information, educational, entertainment, and cultural services to all of its users. If children were directors and participating in a real–life planning and design project, they could develop a sense of societal responsibility and learn what it means to be involved.

Library buildings that provide effectively for the wide range of interests and the tastes of users are not always easy to design. Libraries should provide both traditional and newer facilities and recognize children's expectations for building and designing as imperative. Planning for changing student needs and information technology will be the key factors in planning new buildings. The libraries which contributed to this study should be incorporating the children's expectations into the design of their buildings.

This study provides library planners and practitioners with information on how new library buildings should be designed and, more importantly, how they will be used. Data from libraries in this study illustrate how the new attributes and functions of spaces recorded add value to children's and school library's missions. As a result the library's role will be expanded beyond provision, and access to include a more active role based on the use children see as a priority.

As planning considerations for children's and school libraries change and uses for the physical space become more varied, the library's role in providing children's services is enhanced and extended. This study also provides library planners, authorities and practitioners with data on planning factors, usage, space characteristics, and other design elements to support decision-making as they consider new library buildings for children's services, or equally important, evaluate how existing space is used. While the information revolution will continue to change the way the library approaches its more traditional roles of resources and services, it is clear from this project that incorporating users' views will ensure greater success in meeting children's expectations.

References

Anderson, Dorothy J. 1987. From idealism to realism: Library directors and library services. *Library Trends* 35(3): 393-412.

Banduric, Pamela T. 1993. *Environmental design and the promotion of reading in the children's public library.* (A thesis for the degree of Master of Arts, Michigan State University).

Boone, M. D. 2002. "Library design – the architect's view". *Library Hi Tech* 20 (3): 388-392.

Campbell, D.E. and Shlechter, T.M. 1979. "Library design influences on user behaviour and satisfaction". *Library Quarterly* 49 (1): 26-41.

Cooper, M. and Matthews, A. 2000. *Color smart: How to use color to enhance your business and personal life.* New York, NY: Pocket Books.

Edwards, H. 1990. *University library building planning.* Metuchen, NJ: The Scarecrow Press.

Foote, Steven M. 2004. "Changes in library design: An architect's perspective". *Portal: Libraries and the Academy* 4 (1): 41-59.

Goulding, Anne. 2009. "*The rise, fall and rise of the British public library building.*" 2008. In 17th annual BOBCATSSS symposium (Bobcatsss 2009), Porto (Portugal), 28–30. January 2009. URL: http://eprints.rclis.org/handle/10760/12939?mode=full [viewed September 2011].

IFLA. Libraries for Children and Young Adults Section. 2003. Guidelines for Children's Libraries Services. URL: http://www.ifla.org/VII/s10/pubs/ChildrensGuidelines.pdf [viewed September 2011].

Jenkins, Christine A. 2000. The history of youth services librarianship: A review of the research literature. *Libraries and Culture* 35 (1): 103-140.

Koontz, Christie M. 2007. "A history of location of U.S. public libraries within community place and space: evolving implications for the library's mission of equitable service". *Public Library Quarterly* 26 (1 / 2): 75-100.

Miller, W. 2002. "The library as a place. Tradition and evolution". *Library Issues* 22 (3):1-4.

Önal, H.Inci. 2009. "IFLA / UNESCO School Library Manifesto for creating one world: Germany, Iran and Turkey in comparative perspective". *Libri* 59 (1): 45-54.

Önal, H.Inci. 2006. "Türkiye'de Basımcılık ve Yayıncılığın Bilgi Hizmetlerine Etkisi: Tarihsel Araştırma [The effect of printing and publishing on information services in Turkey: A historical survey]. *Bilgi Dünyasi* [Information World] 2006 7 (1): 1-22.

Önal, H.Inci. 2005. "New developments on the Turkish school library scene". *Journal of Librarianship and Information Science* 37 (3): 141-152.

Önal, H.Inci. 1995. "School library development in Turkey". *Turk Kutuphaneciligi* 9(3): 255- 257.

Rohlf, Robert H. 1986. "Library design: what not to do". *American Libraries* 17 (Issue no if pos rather than monthFebruary): 100-104.

Sannwald, W. W. 2007. "Designing libraries for customers". *Library Administration and Management* 21 (3): 131-138.

Sannwald, W. W. 1997. *Checklist of library building design consideration.* Chicago: American Library Association.

Turkiye Cumhuriyeti Kültür Bakanlığı. 1981. Halk kütüphaneleri görev ve çalışma yönetmeliği [Public libraries bylaw]. T.C. *Resmi Gazete* 21.9.1981. Sayi: 17465.

Turkiye Cumhuriyeti Maarif Vekaleti. 1959. *Okul kutuphaneleri yönetmeligi* [School libraries bylaw]. Ankara: Maarif Basimevi.

Turkiye Cumhuriyeti Milli Egitim Bakanligi. 2009. *2010 Yili butce raporu* [Budget report for the year 2009]. Ankara:Devlet Kitaplari Mudurlugu Basimevi.

Turkiye Cumhuriyeti Milli Egitim Bakanligi. 2006. *Okul kutuphaneleri standart yönergesi* [Standards for school libraries] URL: http://yayim.meb.gov.tr/y%F6netmelik.doc [viewed September 2011].

Turkiye Cumhuriyeti Milli Egitim Bakanligi. 2001. Okul kutuphaneleri yönetmeligi [School libraries bylaw]. *Resmi Gazete*, No. 24501.

Turkiye Cumhuriyeti Milli Egitim Bakanligi.1976. Okul Kutuphaneleri Yönetmeligi [School libraries bylaw]. *Resmi Gazete*, No.15689.

Programme: Jacksonville Public Library Children's and Teens' Libraries

Alex Lamis

Partner, Robert A. M. Stern Architects, New York, USA
and

Barbara A.B. Gubbin

Director, Jacksonville Public Library, Florida, USA

Architectural Intentions

What is the role of physical library buildings in the increasingly digital world of information? What value can these buildings bring to their communities that will justify the expense of their creation and upkeep? How can children's and teens' libraries, through their very design, act as places of learning and as local landmarks? These questions were very much on our minds as we designed a large new central library building in Jacksonville, Florida.

Jacksonville is America's thirteenth largest city[1] and is situated on a semi-tropical plain in the northeast corner of Florida. It is approximately forty miles from St. Augustine, the oldest permanent European settlement in the United States, more than half a century older than the better-known Jamestown and Plymouth colonies. Jacksonville emerged after the Civil War as the terminus of major railroad lines, was an early winter resort, and became a major centre of the pulp and paper industry. Its situation along the broad, tidal St. John's River also made it an ideal location for a significant United States naval base.

In 2005, the city of Jacksonville opened a 30,000-square-meter, new Central Library on Hemming Plaza, a principal square in the centre of the city. Built as part of a visionary public building programme known as the Better Jacksonville Plan, which also called for new courthouses, stadia, parks, and roadways, the new library replaced a building from the 1960s that no longer met the needs of this growing sun-belt city. With a total project cost of approximately $100 million (US), the library represented a significant commitment on the part of the city leadership to education and the advancement of the library system into the 21st century. It was also one of the largest library expansions in the United States in the past decade. In addition to the central library,

---

1   By population (US Census Bureau, 2008)

a number of new and rehabilitated library branches were constructed throughout the city, as part of the Better Jacksonville Plan.

The natural landscape of the region is rich in animals and vegetation ranging from sea-going manatees and blue crabs to alligators and owls, and with mixed forests of pine and cabbage palm. Urban sprawl in this automobile-dependent city has in many cases cut off children and teens from the rich natural landscape. Connecting to, and celebrating, the landscape thus became a primary driver of the interior design of the new Children's Library.

In the teen's library, a similarly thematic approach to design was employed. In this case the design evoked a fantasy, reinterpreting seaside waves as a dynamic flowing ceiling, along with a futuristic environment evoking "cones of silence" and space-age furniture.

Building Design

The design of the library came about as the result of an international design competition with the design of Robert A. M. Stern Architects selected from among four finalists. The competition phase extended for four months and included several intermediate working sessions with stake-holders, including library staff and administration, the library governing board, and members of the city administration, under the guidance of a professional competition advisor. During these work sessions, and through the development of the building programme, the desires of the staff, and especially those relating to children's and teens' services, were taken into consideration.

Once the competition phase was completed and selection of the design team had been made, additional meetings with library staff and administration developed the details of the children's and teens' sections of the library. These areas had been underserved in the existing building, and provision of high-quality library services for children and teens was a priority of the mayor and his administration.

The goal of the design of the library, including the children's and teens' spaces, was to create a series of inviting environments that would reflect the diversity of Jacksonville and would be welcoming to a broad section of the community. As a result, there is no single overarching aesthetic approach within the building but rather a series of distinct "places" that each cater to different groups: retired people, parents with young children, workers, students, researchers, and others. There are also common gathering spaces where the entire community can come together as a group.

The five-story building was planned around a central stair and atrium space, and an exterior but secure courtyard that organized the large building footprint. Different departments are entered off these central spaces, with the more active, louder spaces closer to the main entrance and quieter, more contemplative rooms at the upper levels.

The Children's Library

The building programme called for an 1800-square-metre library for children ranging from toddlers to "tweens" – up to approximately twelve years of age. This wide range of ages necessitated the division of the space into zones catering for different age groups. However, the design of the entire Children's Library has an overarching thematic consistency.

In the early stages of the design process it was determined that in order to attract and interest the maximum number of children, who today grow up in a media-saturated environment, the design of the space should have thematic con-content – it should "tell a story" that was specific and widely accessible. Several different narrative concepts for the space were explored, including 'water world,' 'through the trees,' and 'fantasy-land'. Through a series of discussions these ideas were recombined and a narrative grew from the specific geography and natural history of the Jacksonville region, situated along the Atlantic coast in semi-tropical lowlands which include both forest and water. Jacksonville is home to lush vegetation and a wide variety of birds, animals and fish. While there is a strong sentiment for the preservation of this natural beauty, the pressures of a rapidly growing population and heavy industry put a strain on this environment. The Children's Library celebrates the natural beauty of the region.

Children enter through a 2-metre-high sculptural rendition of

Figure 1. Children's "Through the Grasses" entrance – Peter Aaron / Esto

the high swamp grasses that line the many inland waterways and can imagine themselves to be small animals or bugs crawling through the grass. Lighting and a looped tape recording of natural sounds reinforce the experience. Inside the Library the colours of the floors and walls reflect the dappled green and blue of the environment. Round "porthole" windows between the main space and subsidiary creative labs give the feeling of being underwater.

Figure 2. Alligator sofa in Toddler Story and Play area – Peter Aaron / Esto

Robert A. M. Stern Architects worked together with the local fabricator, Sally's Corporation, to design and build custom furniture in the shapes of local plants and animals: a large circular bench in the form of an alligator, another in the form of a manatee, a third shaped like a boat. There are chairs that look like leaves, turtles, and snails, and small tables that take the form of mushrooms.

An enclosed theatre for story-telling programmes takes the form of a screened-in porch. When children enter the theatre they seem to be in an outdoor room, and lush sculptural plants can be seen "outside." As the lights dim, night appears to fall, and a chorus of insects and frogs can be heard. An "audio-animatronic" or robotic owl, which appears to move and speak, welcomes the children and tells stories.

Computers are seamlessly integrated into the Children's Library, with programmes selected by the staff to be age-appropriate. Traditional library services, and especially books, are not diminished but augmented by the addition of electronic technology. The Children's Library was designed to accommodate new technologies or other opportunities that may present themselves in the future.

Teens' Library

The Teens' Library evokes the atmosphere of a cool clubhouse: a place very different from either home or school; a place that will act as a draw for notoriously finicky American teenagers.

The Teens' Library is located on the ground floor of the five-storey building, easily accessible from the front door, purposefully placed immediately adjacent to the popular materials collection, which will also attract teens. The Popular Materials area has a bookstore feel with casual seating, music listening

Figure 3. Popular Materials Area features music, books, and magazines used often by teens –
Peter Aaron / Esto

stations, a dropped grid of spotlights, movable book and material cases, and a youthful sense of colour and design.

As with the Children's Library, a series of thematic options were presented to the Library; in this case they were 'Life's a Beach'; 'Pop and Funk,' featuring Pop Art and 1960's images; and 'Hit the Road,' derived from the American infatuation with the open road as well as the information super-highway. By mixing and matching these themes the final 'vibe' of the teen room was developed. The Teens' Library is entered through a covered threshold separate from the rest of the library that gives it a distinct identity. Bold, wave-like ceiling elements give the space a dynamic quality and are rendered in bold bright colours. An over-scaled seating area with a long couch, sofa, and chairs encourages casual conversations among as many as a dozen teens. Video displays are distributed throughout the space; in order to control and limit unwanted noise coming from the displays, sound is channelled through semi-spherical "cones of silence" to the individual user. The desk on duty is prominently located so the librarian can monitor all activities in the space as well as support teens by answering their questions, assisting with technical issues, and proactively helping with homework projects. There are informal seating groups with café-style seats and magazine racks, banks of computer stations, and more private, quieter areas for study. Classic modern furniture by Charles Eames and others, salvaged from the 1960's library, was re-used in the Teens' Library.

Public libraries face an increasingly complex challenge today of remaining relevant and engaged in a world of new and quickly-evolving media formats. The architectural and interior design of a library play an important role in this challenge by facilitating the use of library resources to help patrons navigate the variety of new and traditional media and making the library feel like a welcoming space for all members of its community. With the design for the Jacksonville Public Library's children's and teens' spaces, Robert A.M. Stern Architects aimed to make the library a friendly and accessible space for learning, collaboration, expression, and creation that would draw people back again and again.

After the Opening...

The new Main Library, which opened in November 2005, was an instant success with over 13,000 people attending the official opening. In the year before the new Main Library opened, circulation of teen and children's materials from the Main Library was 61,878 items; in 2009 circulation had increased to 411,464 items. Programming for teens which had been almost non-existent (57 programmes in a year) increased to 376 programmes and attendance at children's programming increased by 177% with over 5,000 participants.

Location of the new Main Library cannot be a major factor propelling this significant growth in use because the new facility is located only three blocks from the former Main Library, which you can see from the windows. This is a downtown location, in an area which has very limited housing, few schools nearby, and tends to "close-up" in the evening and weekends despite continuing efforts by businesses and the city to encourage more downtown visitors. Despite what might be considered "obstacles" the Main Library has been an overwhelming success in the community. The oft-repeated adage "Build it and they will come" rings true in Jacksonville. People respond positively to the building's design, its warmth and its zing, as well as the programmes and services which are offered. Responding to the online customer survey, Jacksonville residents regularly tell us that they bring visiting guests to the classically-designed, imposing 30,000 square metre building to show it off. The conference centre and open courtyard – this is Florida after all and we celebrate being the "Sunshine State"– are popular venues for meetings, receptions, parties and weddings; there is a café, and also a bookstore operated by the Friends of the Library. And there are the specially designed and dedicated teen and children's spaces, each with their own clientele, who come from all over Jacksonville. The Main Library has become a destination in the true sense of that word.

The Teen Library: What Works!

The design, as Alex Lamis has described, is "cool clubhouse" but also timeless. The bright colours, the curvy ceiling design, the large couch and comfortable furnishings do not "date" the space; they attract young people and since the design is like no other space in the building it becomes "their" space. The location was deliberately chosen to be adjacent to the popular materials collection and away from the Children's Library which is on the floor above, and has its own entrance using glass doors. No other department in the building has doors for its entryway – another distinguishing feature which allows for noise management as well as emphasizing the special nature of the space.

Figure 4. Teen services area – Lounge seating clusters allow for casual interactions – Peter Aaron / Esto

Our teen customers enjoy the stereo system with surround sound and TV screens. There are 13 computers which have been sufficient so far and teens can bring in their own laptops if they have them as the entire building has Wi-Fi capability. When funds are available we will consider adding laptops to check out and use in the space as many of the teens who come downtown do not have computers of their own, yet want to manage their Facebook and MySpace pages and get on the web.

Library staff gives high marks to the space design which allows them to monitor the teen library space effectively from their desk – there is very little "dead" space. We ask all our customers to follow a posted Code of Conduct and do not tolerate poor behaviour. Staff wear wireless phones to communicate with customers and can also call security if necessary. This dispels any concern there could be about the location of the Teen Library away from the main traffic pattern and operating in an enclosed space.

There are two study rooms. Early on there were plans to put snack and drink machines in one of these to make a quasi café but this was not done. We do allow covered drinks in the Teen Library and with a café in our library lobby, the staff are generally pleased we did not go ahead with the food machines. Both rooms are used as conference rooms and often as quiet spaces. The latter is important and appreciated by the teens. We allow cell phone use in the library and the teen space which, because it is used by teens, can be noisy. However, we find most teens monitor themselves with little staff intervention.

Regular shelving provides access to print materials, magazines, and media. We also have a large comic book and manga collection which circulates. There is a dedicated staff for this space, two professional librarians, one of whom is the manager, two paraprofessionals and a clerk. There is a staff work room immediately accessible from the staff desk in the teen room with work spaces for each staff member and access to a larger shared work space to work on projects requiring a sink or large table to spread out material.

The Teen Room: What Have We Learned?

Be mobile – be flexible. The space we have is sufficient, almost 400 square metres, which gives a level of intimacy to the space which teens appreciate. Any large scale teen activities, the annual Battle of the Bands for example, are held in our conference centre which includes meeting rooms and an auditorium with comfortable seating for 400 people. However, teen space must be flexible. It is used for a very broad range of activities – groups and individuals using the computers, listening to music, reading, playing Go!, making crafts, drawing and painting, writing, watching movies, talking, playing games on the computers, doing homework, and participating in our electronic classroom with programmes such as "Pizza and Pursuit of Resources" which teaches information literacy skills. If we were to reconfigure the space today we would put as much as we could on wheels to make it mobile and flexible. Let the teen furniture be "big" – teens love this – but easy to move around. You should also anticipate that teens enjoy sitting on the floor; space and furnishings to support this are important. Today we would certainly greatly reduce the size of the staff desk and make it mobile as well for added flexibility. Be flexible in terms of technology and equipment. Do not invest in any technology, equipment or furniture which cannot withstand heavy use or be repaired easily. This is simple to say but difficult to do when in the middle of a major design project and funds are there to install new furnishings and new gadgetry. Our listening stations for example, which are attached to the wall, are frequently out of order and in today's world when most teens have iPods or mp3 players are these really necessary?

Teens Love to Show Off! Provide more display space than you would expect the teens to need and then some more. In addition to staff displays of books and media, calendars and event announcements, our teens are always making things, writing poetry on the magnetic poetry board, drawing and painting – they want to display it all on both vertical and horizontal surfaces – at the same time! New and different displays both involve teens in their own space – we have a teen council which helps us plan programmes and activities – and attract teens to the space to see what is "on display." The space design should make the most of this marketing opportunity.

What Else Do Teens Want?

What else would our teens and staff like in their teen space? When I asked this question answers included an aquarium, a dance floor, a videogame console, collaborative workstations to allow two to three teens to work together at a single computer, and a recording studio. The teens also want their own self-check out station like those we have at the main circulation desk and in the Children's Library to check out their own materials. If your space design is flexible and your furniture mobile you can implement many if not all these ideas after you have opened for service – a study room to a recording studio and shelves moved for a portable dance floor for example.

From a single range of bookshelves in a corridor at the "old" Main Library, located there for lack of any other space, teen services have come a long way at the Jacksonville Public Library and much of this can be attributed to designating and designing a space with teens in mind.

The Children's Library: How do you spell S-U-C-C-E-S-S?

For many of our customers the Children's Library is the greatest success story of our new Main Library. Parents and grandparents come from all over town to bring their children and grandchildren to toddler time, stories with Mrs Owl, bilingual story hour (French, Portuguese and Spanish), arts and crafts, and special programmes such as guitar lessons and creative writing classes. Children come during the week from day care centres and schools. Often the children and caregivers eat lunch in our open-air courtyard adjacent to the Children's Library after attending a children's programme. The adjacency of the Children's Library with its "environmental" theme to the courtyard adds a significant extra dimension to the capacity of the children's space to accommodate groups – and at different times in the day.

Figure 5. Interior of "Underwater" Activity Room – Peter Aaron / Esto

This Children's Library is easily eight times larger than in the previous library
and the design theme, which reflects the environment of northeast Florida, is

timeless. With its blue and green "outdoor" colours, anthropomorphic furnishings and low shelving the Children's Library, just like the teen space is clearly meant for children. It is their space.

The various designated spaces are well used and allow for programming concurrently for different groups. There are two arts and crafts rooms with sinks, flooring which can be easily cleaned, work spaces and child-sized furniture. With dedicated art space and an artist on the staff this makes for imaginative and creative programming. The Children's Theatre, which hosts Mrs Owl, is used by staff and performance groups for story hour. It works particularly well for toddler time as the floor is carpeted and the low light provides a sense of intimacy. It also hosts sing-alongs, classes and plays.

The Children's Library has a self service checkout machine installed after the library had been open for two years, a great hit with kids and parents alike. It saves parents having to queue up or juggle books and children in the circulation area downstairs, and children are fearless when it comes to technology and demand that even the most technology averse parent let them use it! There are sixteen computers for children placed on child-sized furniture, which are well used.

What Have We Learned?

The Children's Library would benefit from a space specifically designed for babies with comfortable seating so that parents could both watch their children and visit between themselves. In another of our libraries we have designed a "baby-space" which has been very well received and staff report that mothers linger longer in the library as a result.

The large-scale furniture, the couches designed as an alligator and a manatee as well as a boat for a family reading space, are attractive and well-used. However, the surfaces are too hard for the smallest children to play and climb on. The concept is very appealing but providing a softer surface would mean less monitoring of the furniture by staff concerned for child safety.

When I asked the staff what changes or additions they would like to see in this space better to accommodate their young customers, their answers included more display space for children's art and crafts, a space for nursing mothers to have some privacy, and a family restroom for use by parents and children of either sex though they did note that the child-sized furnishings in the two children's restrooms are much appreciated.

The staff desk in this area has not been as successful as in the teen area. The Children's Library, which runs the length of one side of the building is long rather than wide and placement of the staff desk so that it is easily accessible to the staff work area but set back from the entrance to the department is problematic in terms of viewing the whole space. Our answer has been to install mirrors and institute a staff roaming programme. Now in place throughout the Main Library but begun in the Children's Library, this has the staff roaming the space to provide assistance with finding materials or using the computers, but also to ensure that children are not "lost" and to provide an extra level of security.

One final comment from the manager of the Children's Library is to provide a globe in the children's area. The one in the Children's Library has been so heavily used over the past four years with little fingers finding Jacksonville that Florida is now completely worn away!

End of this Story ... or perhaps this is just the Beginning.

Teen and children's libraries should be places for exploration whether in books, online or in person, interacting with other children, teens and family members. Designing your library's space for youth services to enhance a young person's sense of adventure so that it is fun to visit and provides the opportunity for a different adventure each time will attract children, teens and their families to libraries as it has done to the Main Library in Jacksonville, literally in the thousands.

Relevant Links

The Better Jacksonville Plan: http://www.jaxjazzfest.org/Departments/Better+Jacksonville+Plan/default.htm [viewed September 2011].

Jacksonville Public Library: http://jpl.coj.net/ [viewed September 2011].

Robert A.M. Stern Architects: http://www.ramsa.com [viewed September 2011].

RAMSA Projects: Jacksonville Public Library: http://www.ramsa.com/project.aspx?id=83 [viewed September 2011].

Santiago Public Library: A Challenge for Children and Young Adults

Gonzalo Oyarzún
National Coordinator of the Public Libraries System of Chile and Member of Libraries, Archives and Museums Directorate of Chile (DIBAM)

Introduction

The design of the library for children and young adults in Santiago had a number of aims at the outset of the planning process. These were that the children and young person's library should be:

- created as a public square, where children and youngsters could go and have fun.
- created as a public space, where children and youngsters could feel free to choose, explore and learn.
- an intimate place where children and youngsters can meet and interact with others, assuming and respecting their differences and times.
- a place where parents and children can talk and get to know each other.
- an environment in which teachers and students can work and experience learning together far removed from the pressure and restrictions of the school curriculum.
- a multimedia and interactive zone where children have free access to
- books, new technologies, activities, highly trained professionals, comfortable furniture and a, state-of-the-art infrastructure all at the right scale and with adequate opening hours –and always with the opportunity to listen to a good story.
- above all be a truly impressive experience.

Public libraries are increasingly assuming the task of making children's libraries less scholarly and more fun. They have a different role in the learning and development process to that of schools. Their aim is to take a more integral approach, improving personal competencies through encouraging the young to read. In this approach, the motivation comes from the pleasure of reading rather than measuring a level of reading comprehension. To achieve this libraries have to make adjustments in design and spatial planning to encourage children and youngsters to feel at home in the library environment. The library, therefore, must adapt to the needs of children and youngsters, and not vice versa.

These are the principles which formed the basis for the design of Santiago Public Library's children's spaces.

Santiago Public Library

With over 400 public libraries throughout the country, in addition to other lending places such as *cajas viajeras* ("travelling boxes"), *bibliobuses, bibliometros* (subway-station-based lending places), and also hospital and prison libraries, Chile has an extensive book lending network with, however, very unequal collections and infrastructure. Chile does not have a model public library, which can demonstrate the potential of such facilities as is more common in countries with a more profound history and development in libraries.

Biblioteca di Santiago, Chile   Consultants: VITETTA Architects: Cox y Ugarte

Figure 1. Santiago Public Library, Chile.

Located in the Chilean capital, Santiago Public Library was opened in November 11th, 2005. It proposed a revolutionary concept for Chile, offering innovative methods of service delivery. These included longer opening hours, including weekends; digital reference services, audiovisual collections and novel services; and collections for children, teenagers and adults as well as, reference, and general literature collections. In addition the library has computer halls equipped to train users in the new information and communication technologies (*ICTs*); integral disabled access at every service point; a multifunctional auditorium; exhibition halls; and well-established programmes to encourage reading and literacy.

This 22.000 m^2 (236.806 sq.ft.) library aims to bring a modern and efficient public library service to the whole community which is different from the National Library (*Biblioteca Nacional*) and which will be part of the national public library network. From its inception, it has been established both as an experimental service and the model for the development of other libraries in the country. Santiago Public Library provides a service to a region with more than six million inhabitants, demanding more access to reading and information day by day.

The library has approximately a million visits every year and children and young adults are essentially the main users, representing more than 65% of the total number of visitors. This is no random occurrence: the library is located in a neighbourhood with a significant number of schools and daycare centres. It is also located near major private and public transport routes with two subway stations from different lines being in very close proximity to the building.

Design

Anticipating the challenge, the design stage for the children's and young person's library was very intense and involved many different professionals. Work was focused in three areas: architecture, design and community.

The building in which the Library is located used to be a state warehouse. Although such a building might be thought to provide plenty of room and flexibility due to its sizeable halls and open spaces, the remodelling was limited to certain existing spaces. It was agreed that the focus of the design should be on the user in a constantly changing environment. Flexibility was the key with rooms, and spaces in the building able to be modified as required. The library has been constructed with a view to possible and future uses – human as well as technological.

This is particularly important when considering an infant and juvenile library where change is impacting on everything from the materials used to the way adults relate to the youth of today. Much has changed in the last thirty years and thus it can be assumed that things will be very different again in another thirty years. The role children and young people have today in the country's activities and political decision making and the level of participation they have in schools, the family, or indeed the city must be taken into account when designing a library service to meet their needs. In addition technological advances and transformation in the national educational and cultural scene must be considered when designing and building such facilities.

Biblioteca di Santiago, Chile   Consultants: VITETTA Architects: Cox y Ugarte

Figure 2. Children's reading area

The interior design also has to take flexibility into account. Graphic and interior designers need to give thought to suitable furniture, signage, and colour. Children's libraries must be developed in such a way that users can find the information they need intuitively and by topic rather than by learning to interpret numeric and alphabetical codes.

Most of the library users belong to the poorest areas of the city. In their small and generally overcrowded houses, there is unlikely to be adequate space for comfortable study or leisure activities. Therefore, it is all the more important for the library to be a comfortable and cosy space, an extension to their home, and a place they can feel is their own.

The library should not be all about prohibition and what users should not do – talking, even speaking aloud is permitted, eating a sandwich or drinking a soda is accepted as well. Why not? One might, for instance, think such practices may damage a book, but if a child or teenager cannot do that in the library then he or she will borrow the book, take it home, lie down on his or her bed, have a sandwich and a drink, and read the book in comfort there. The policy in Santiago Public Library differs by far from such a restrictive approach: education through use is encouraged rather than implementing bans. It is better for children to be in the library, which is likely to be a more comfortable place. It is the task of the library staff to teach children not to damage the books and share them with others.

Biblioteca di Santiago, Chile   Consultants: VITETTA Architects: Cox y Ugarte

Figure 3. Mixed activity area

Feedback was obtained from the local community who were asked what kind of infant and juvenile library they expected or needed. A year before the inauguration, meetings were held with teachers, parents, and specialists in order to learn about their expectations and understanding of such a facility. Also interviews were held with children and teenagers so they could tell us, or illustrate through drawings, how their ideal library should look. Important decisions were then based on these findings.

Having gathered all the data, the librarians started to organize and prepare the books, materials, and services which the new library should provide. As mentioned above, the decision was taken to organize the information thematically rather than arranging material according to numeric and alphabetical codes. As a result thematic areas were created so any child or youngster could quickly grasp the layout and find material required. This approach was very different to the Dewey Decimal System of classification which is by far the most commonly used in Chile.

The infant and juvenile committees selected the best available books, computers were programmed appropriate to the age of the various user groups, and appealing activities for children and young people were planned. Such activities took the role of accompanying parents or teachers into account.

The library staff structure changed too. The configuration of interdisciplinary teams was a keystone of the success of the project. Librarians, teachers at all levels, entertainers, performers, story-tellers, sketch artists, and a large team consisting of both paid and voluntary personnel were essential to implement the new library service.

Children's Library

Deemed mainly for children aged 0 to 8, this is a playful area with its main purpose being to give free rein to the imagination and including well defined areas for babies, infants, and children. It aims to be a space for entertainment, where children have access to books and develop their imagination through games. Everything has been carefully thought out: the areas for babies are provided with appropriate spaces for pushchairs and some collections of interest to parents as well as for the infants. The ambience should be similar in a way to that of a park.

In this room there is a space dedicated to early readers, from 0 to 3 years old, – "Born to Read" – where together with their parents they can share reading, games and toys. This allows the development of an artistic, recreational or educational nature. This area has nappy-changing tables and toilets with the correct dimensions and designs for younger children. The room also has an audiovisual section and another place for story time, infant theatre, and a puppet show. As a basic concept for the whole room, every component is movable in order to create new environments as required.

Youth Library

Connected to the infant area through an interior stair, this room is the logical continuation of the previous one. Its collections are focused on children aged 8 to 16, and it aims to intensify their imagination and enjoyment for reading.

It can be defined as an informal educational space, in which the young people can explore a world of new possibilities through reading, literature workshops, theatre, films, the Internet, role-playing games and other activities.

Its setting has been specially designed to offer the young users a place which invites them in and welcomes them: playful, relaxed, without the formality of traditional reading rooms. It has sections for audiovisual material, literature workshops, and theatre. It also has touch screens and audiovisual channel circuits for projecting films and documentaries.

Figure 4.Teenagers' reading area

Impact of the new library

With the opening of Santiago Public Library, public libraries have started to be considered as relevant places in national matters. Public libraries are part of

Figure 5. Storytelling

the political and economic agenda of the country. Key meetings relating to childhood, youth, and secondary level students take place in our facilities. Thus, Santiago Public Library has become a benchmark in public policy. The Chilean President, Michelle Bachelet, has passed a law which states that all districts lacking a library will have one before the end of 2010.

Nowadays those libraries are being built on the Santiago Public Library model thus providing facilities for children and young people which are an essential element of education, culture and participation.

The Red Thread in Hjoerring

Tone Lunden
Children's librarian and children's library consultant
at Hjoerring Libraries; Denmark

Two milk, one dress, a pillow and three books – "shopping" in the library and a library in a shopping centre.

In 2007 we were guaranteed a new central library, situated in a shopping centre with 40 shops. We invited the artist duo Bosch & Fjord, whose mutual wish is to integrate art as a natural part of our everyday lives and combine art, design and architecture in their work, to collaborate with us. Their intention was to make the library in Hjoerring "the pivotal point of the town". We also invited Lammhults Library Design, a firm with international experience in fitting out library interiors, to work with us.

Thoughts, visions, experiences and inspiration were mixed together, and we drew up the final plans in August 2007 and then opened in April 2008. We imagined the library as a theatre – 'the stage' as the place where the users meet the magic of the library and have the opportunity to interact; 'the store of set pieces' to make interesting changes and provide 'the backstage' for the staff.

As well as drawing on theatres for ideas we were inspired by the way museums, science centres and similar places mediate and interact with their customers. We thought in terms of the library as one of "The great good places" mentioned by Ray Oldenburg[1] and also gleaned inspiration from the Danish architect Jan Gehl and his ideas about multiplicity and diversity in city planning.

The library is the central library in a municipality with 67.102 inhabitants and we have 4 branches and a mobile library as well. The central library has a Tourist Information Centre and this also gives us new opportunities – and customers.

---

1 Oldenburg, Ray (1991) *The Great Good Place*. New York: Marlowe & Company.

Figure 1. The red thread

The library's identity is based on the red thread which winds through the rooms like veins of blood. Going up and down, through and under, sometimes over a bench, sometimes shelves, a table, a desk or places for exhibitions. The red thread is made of wood except from the part in the floor. We use this red thread also for mediating – this can be people recommending books or books about how to survive the financial crisis.

We have many different kinds of furniture for sitting down – alone or in a group. We have quiet zones and activity zones and no borders between sections for different ages. The library is in one room but contains many 'rooms' with different expressions and the red thread links all the different parts.

In the welcome area the user finds new books and other media for all ages, a lounge with screens in different sizes for TV showing exhibitions or weather forecasts. Here too is the Tourist Information Centre, the café and the area for borrowing/lending and information. Further on are study rooms, theme niches in a vivid orange colour for exhibitions, a TV lounge, bookcases, from floor to ceiling, displaying books or magazines like a bookstore and with ladders to climb up.

All our media are on open shelves – nothing is stored away in basements. In the area with older books the setting changes from modern white decor to mahogany and Chesterfield chairs.

Figure 2. Slide bookcase

In the children's department we wanted to express even more the idea that experience includes the whole body. As a symbol we placed a 'slide-bookcase' (a mix of a slide from a playground and bookshelves) in the middle of the library. We have areas for action and areas with a bit more silence – like the Reading Tubes. It is also evident that children have opportunities to express themselves.

Figure 3. Interactive area

We have participated in different Nordic projects like "Leaving Marks" with support from Nordic Culture Point and a Danish project "Children's library as an exploratory". Experience from these projects was integrated in this new library.

We have inter alia been inspired by Howard Gardner's theory about the multiple intelligences[2] and Sven Nilsson's pyramid of cultural needs[3].

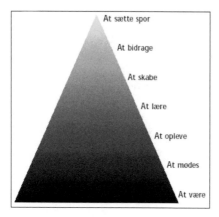

Figure 4. Nilsson's pyramid

In the figure, from top to bottom: To leave one's mark, To contribute, To create, To learn, To experience, To meet, To be.

We would like to offer all the steps in this pyramid in our library taking into consideration that children learn and experience in different ways. We would like to use curiosity and fascination in our approach. The children visit the library of their own volition, and we never know how many will be coming or how long they will be staying. Naturally, some come with their school, their kindergarten or their family, but quite a lot of children/youngsters come alone or together with friends. The Danish researcher into play culture, Carsten Jessen, has said that the children's library is one of the few places where play culture thrives whatever the age of the user, and we see this as a rather exciting challenge.

---

2   Gardner, Howard (1993) *Multiple Intelligences: New Horizons*. New York: Basic Books.
3   In Swedish: http://www.polyvalent.se/framtidsfilerna/meningen.html [viewed September 2011].
     In English: http://archive.ifla.org/IV/ifla69/papers/002e-Buchhave.pdf [viewed September 2011].

Figure 5. Children's area

In relation to the creative process and making marks we have for example the Animator and the Critic. In the Animator you can create short animation films and then watch them on a big screen. We currently change the animated figures; they might be animals, knights or circus performers and the children themselves decide the length and title of their film. In the Critic you make a video recording of something you are interested in. This might be a summer holiday event, a film, a song or a book you want to recommend. This is also shown on a big screen. In this way children's 'stories' become part of the library, which is regarded as the house of stories. You can also play with words and rhymes in the Hair-splitter, which is placed next to books on the same subject.

Everywhere in the library we have various carefully thought out places to relax – with sofas, bar stools, easy chairs and also in the children's library a large 'Puddle' where you can read comfortably by yourself or with your class. Dressing up clothes and masks are a big hit! The costumes we bought initially turned out to be too small, as older children and youngsters also wanted to dress up. We are always on the look-out for exciting toys of the kind that encourage children to explore and things that will get a conversation going.

Figure 6. Picture book area

The area for picture books is constructed like a park with a tree, so all year round you can sit or lie in the park reading books. That is very nice with a climate like the Danish one!

The VIP (Very Important Parents) lounge has magazines and books about children, but also about gardening, marriage, cars and knitting.

Figure 7. Parents' lounge

We have a big area for exhibitions and different workshops – for example painting for children of different ages. There we have theatre amps, projectors, screens, scaffolding, costumes and other equipment. We work with themes like Colour Yellow, Trolls, Birds and Frogs, Sculptures and we cooperate with teachers and artists.

In connection with a nature exhibition, for example, there might be stuffed birds and you could also see pictures from the countryside, listen to birdsong and draw and paint birds. During the school holidays, on weekday afternoons or on Saturday mornings, we often arrange open workshops, where the theme varies according to which exhibition we are showing or they might relate to the seasons – Easter, Christmas etc. With 'Colour Yellow' we began well in advance to collect yellow objects – a pair of yellow socks, a yellow teapot and later a yellow bicycle or yellow tins. The exhibition grew in size prior to the creative workshop where the children contemplated an object and painted a picture – in yellow, of course. On these occasions all members of staff get involved and make their own contribution.

Figure 8. Creative play

We have our own dinosaur robot: Biblo Pleo. He takes part in a programme where children aged 3-6 years are told stories and facts about dinosaurs. This can in fact be quite difficult, as a lot of children know much more about this subject than adults do. The programme also contains puzzles with dinosaurs, building bricks, excavation a skeleton and finally the children play with Biblo Pleo. Having participated in this programme, a kindergarten took up the theme of dinosaurs – they constructed life-size dinosaurs in a park close by and painted some very attractive pictures. Their process and the pictures were exhibited in the library. In this way both parties contribute something and help to give other visitors a good experience.

From time to time we play Wii on a big screen in the area and we also welcome a major exhibition each year from outside, as for example 'The secret lost property office' from Den 7. Himmel (the 7th heaven)[4] (http://www.7himmel. dk/index.html). An exhibition that inspires guessing games, but also language stimulation and reading. We have previously had the exhibition 'Goldilocks and the three bears' from Børnekulissen in Aarhus. Here you could become part of the fairytale yourself through play, and material was also available for the adults to illustrate how one could use the exhibition for experimenting with the language.

---

4   See 3.

We are fully aware that as a library we need creative people from different professional backgrounds and we work hard on establishing new contacts. The particular challenge seen in a library context is that it is not easy to arrange a longer sequence. We operate more in terms of 'appetizers'. Artists are, as we know, often very competent 'eye-openers' when it comes to other ways in which to experience and express oneself. And art teachers and others possess excellent tools as regards mediation. We would also like to work more with nature and technology, mathematics and other subjects, but still experienced in a cultural context and not in a class room.

The library participates in national as well regional and local initiatives. It may, for example, be in connection with the Danish championship in reading, stimulating a love of reading in the kindergartens or in the preparation of a municipal children's policy. We work together with others on health – how to incorporate an aspect of health in an attractive way via for example music and singing? In connection with the annual Spil Dansk Dag (Play Danish Day), the library takes an active part together with other local organisers and this provides us with new angles, approaches and partners.

In the report from the Danish Agency for Libraries and Media, *Report on future library services to children*[5], which contains 10 recommendations for action, we have been particularly interested in:

– No. 2: The library space must create surprise and inspiration
– No. 4: Children play – in the library
– No. 8: The library supports learning and education.

Play, curiosity and creativity are important keywords both in relation to the library and to the library's content. We can see, for example, that picture books are being used much more than previously, and we attribute this to the fact that this area has a central position and offers opportunities for play and being together to a greater extent than was the case before.

---

5   http://www.splq.info/issues/vol41_3/04.htm [viewed September 2011]

Figure 9. Reading under the tree

In our former library we had separate sections – kids to the left and adults to the right. In the new library we wanted to mix ages and work with keywords for the whole library such as : surprise, interaction, opportunities and new ways of mediating. We have a monthly theme with exhibitions on the red thread with media for all ages, like Greenland or Human Rights. And we often go browsing in the centre for accessories; sometimes we buy to have in stock and sometimes we even borrow. And the location in the 'Metropol – shopping and lifestyle' also gives us new customers. We have approximately 1,200 visitors daily, people of all ages, coming in alone or with school, kindergarten or other groups.The increase in daily users is over 50 % and in loans around 10 – 15 %.

We are now, with grants from the Danish Agency for Library and Media, working with our customers' way of using the library in a project called 'Walking the library'. Here we use RFID and tags combined with interviews to monitor, for example, what people do at the library, where they go and how long they stay. This is a development project in collaboration with Aalborg University and the Royal School of Library and Information Science.

We are very proud to be on the list of the best libraries in Europe[6], as well as of our customers' statements like "we are so happy about our tax money being spent on a place like this" and "this must be a fabulous place to work". And it is!

Figure 10. Reading wall

---

6   http://www.librarybuildings.info/ [viewed September 2011]

http://www.splq.info/issues/vol41_4/07.htm [viewed September 2011]

Facts: http://www.librarybuildings.info/denmark/hjoerring-library-metropol [viewed September 2011]

Video: http://www.bcieurobib.com/hj%C3%B8rring-library-video-featuring-bci-radius-shelving-and-childrens-furniture/ [viewed September 2011]

Timelapse video: http://www.youtube.com/watch?v=3OrO7VQ-N14 [viewed September 2011]

Video: http://www.youtube.com/watch?v=gSAODKQe1QU [viewed September 2011]

Website: www.hjbib.dk [viewed September 2011]

Facebook:

http://www.facebook.com/pages/Hj%C3%B8rring-Bibliotekerne/12640954660 [viewed September 2011]

http://www.rosanbosch.com/#/467341_466865/ [viewed September 2011]

http://www.runefjord.dk/#/471290_470814/ [viewed September 2011]

"Here You Can Go Everywhere You Want, Sort of..." Building a New Children's Library The Library of 100 Talents

Karen Bertrams
Library consultant at ProBiblio; Netherlands
and
Monique Mosch
Advisor for libraries, bookstores and pedagogical institutions; Netherlands
English version: Ria Smith, ProBiblio

In the Library of 100 Talents the children are the librarian. Fundamentally, the library of the future is the result of a process identifying the way children use information, create new contexts and share these with other children. This requires a different type of building, a building that makes it possible to organise and share information in new ways.

Figure 1. Library of 100 Talents

The initiative for a new approach to design came from Rob Bruijnzeels of the Dutch Library Association who said, "In the apparent profusion of information, media, consumption and activities, there is an opportunity for libraries to step up as important questions are being asked: how do we create richness through abundance? What can be judged as true and meaningful information? What makes particular information special to the person taking it in, using it for his or her own purposes? The librarian could play an important role in these questions but in which way? The library of the future seeks answers to these questions and raises new questions. By thinking up and developing new forms of practice and forward-thinking strategies, the library of the future looks ahead without leaving its roots behind." (Bruijnzeels, 2001)

One of the results of building a new children's library in Heerhugowaard, a town North of Amsterdam, The Netherlands, is summarised by a statement in the visitors' book, 'Here you can go everywhere you want, sort of', written down by a child entering the new library for the first time in December 2006.

Figure 2. Model of a children's library

The project started in 2002 when a local school was asked to build a model of a new children's library to be entered in the national contest 'The Library of 100 Talents'. The children entered into the spirit of the competition full of enthusiasm. The school's concept won and the library used the children's ideas to develop the new library that had been planned.

During the process many questions had to be answered. How do children learn, how do they develop their talents? How do schools and, for instance, museums respond to this? How do we translate this into the design of the library? How do architects work, what is the effect of colours, what is essential in the design of a building? What are the talents of our staff, and which skills need to be added to the team?

Figure 3. Chilling out

Many experts from various disciplines worked together to find an answer, not always treading well-known paths and often stumbling in the dark. Working together proved to be absolutely essential in creating the Library of 100 Talents in Heerhugowaard.

Figure 4. Working together

Sources of inspiration

The concept of the Library of 100 Talents finds its roots in the educational visions of Reggio Emilia and the multiple intelligence theory of Howard Gardner.

The Reggio vision, developed since 1945 by the pedagogue Loris Malaguzzi together with teachers and parents, is described as the 100 languages of children. Children can express themselves not only in speech but also in sounds, motions, colours, painting, building, sculpting and many more ways.

Figure 5. Creative play

Based on this vision, educators and artists have been working with young children for decades in the children's centres of Reggio Emilia (Italy). Working together on thoughts, ideas, hypotheses and exchanging memories also offers many positive opportunities in developing the children's library. Children's abilities are the starting point for working with them: how intelligent is the child, what is his or her particular intelligence? The library is traditionally a very 'linguistic' institution, but many children learn and communicate in a non-linguistic manner. The question is: in which way is a child intelligent?

Figure 6. Play table

A poem by Loris Malaguzzi[1]

The child is made of one hundred.
The child has a hundred languages
a hundred hands
a hundred thoughts
a hundred ways of thinking
of playing, of speaking.
A hundred, always a hundred
ways of listening
of marveling
of loving
a hundred joys for singing
and understanding
a hundred worlds to discover
a hundred worlds to invent
a hundred worlds to dream.

---

1   http://www.reggiokids.com/about/hundred_languages.php (retrieved September 2011).

The child has a hundred languages
(and a hundred hundred hundred more)
but they steal ninety-nine
the school and the culture
separate the head from the body.
They tell the child to think
without hands
to do without head
to listen and not speak
to understand without joy
to love and marvel
only at Easter and Christmas.
They tell the child
to discover the world already there
and of the hundred
they steal ninety-nine.
They tell the child that
work and play
reality and fantasy
science and imagination
sky and earth
reason and dream
are things
that do not belong together.
And thus they tell the child
that the hundred is not there.
The child says:
No way. The hundred is there!

The learning theory of Howard Gardner explains how children look at the world in their own way. He distinguishes eight different forms of intelligence:

Linguistic intelligence involves sensitivity to spoken and written language, the ability to learn languages, and the capacity to use language to accomplish certain goals. This intelligence includes the ability to use language effectively, to express oneself rhetorically or poetically; and to use language as a means to remember information. Writers, poets, lawyers and speakers are among those that Howard Gardner sees as having high linguistic intelligence.

Logical-mathematical intelligence consists of the capacity to analyze problems logically, carry out mathematical operations, and investigate issues scientifically. In Howard Gardner's words, it entails the ability to detect patterns, reason deductively and think logically. This intelligence is most often associated with scientific and mathematical thinking.

Musical intelligence involves skill in the performance, composition, and appreciation of musical patterns. It encompasses the capacity to recognize and compose musical pitches, tones, and rhythms. According to Howard Gardner musical intelligence runs in an almost structural parallel to linguistic intelligence.

Bodily-kinesthetic intelligence entails the potential of using one's whole body or parts of the body to solve problems. It is the ability to use mental abilities to coordinate bodily movements. Howard Gardner sees mental and physical activity as related.

Naturalist intelligence enables human beings to recognize, categorize and draw upon certain features of the environment. It combines a description of the core ability with a characterization of the role that many cultures value.

Spatial intelligence involves the potential to recognize and use the patterns of wide space and more confined areas.

Interpersonal intelligence is concerned with the capacity to understand the intentions, motivations and desires of other people. It allows people to work effectively with others. Educators, salespeople, religious and political leaders and counsellors all need a well-developed interpersonal intelligence.

Intrapersonal intelligence entails the capacity to understand oneself, to appreciate one's feelings, fears and motivations. In Howard Gardner's view it involves having an effective working model of ourselves, and to be able to use such information to regulate our lives.
Spiritual, existential and moral intelligence might in the future be included in Gardner's list.

Figure 7. Imagination knows no bounds

Master classes

During the planning and building process of the Heerhugowaard Library the wishes and ideas of the youngest generation about the building, including the look and feel and the programming, particularly of the children's library, were seriously and carefully taken into account. Two-hundred and fifty children, 11/12 year olds from 10 different schools, took part in brainstorming sessions on how the new library should look. In a number of master classes, children from different schools who were interested in a certain subject, worked devotedly and enthusiastically on various relevant issues, together with professionals and librarians. Areas explored included:

- Communication and publicity – how should library staff and children communicate with each other?
- Design – how should the chairs and cupboards and play area furniture look, smell and feel? What functions can they have, besides the obvious ones?
- Website – how could a more attractive, challenging, clear and useful library website be designed?

- Architecture – it was agreed that a scale model of the future library should be built to gain a better insight and understanding of the building.
- Programming – the kind of activities and subjects that should be included were discussed and examined to identify different ways this could be executed.
- System – inventing a new system to present all the different media and their functions and possibilities.

Figure 8. Young Library Users

By recording the results carefully in text, film and illustrations, the architect's brief for the children's library gradually developed, resulting in extraordinary solutions. One of them is a dome on the roof of the 4th floor where the children can have a view over their town.

Figure 9. A place to relax

For many of the professionals involved in these master classes it was an entirely new and inspiring experience.

Collection

The multimedia collection is presented in a number of 'islands' – *things to do, nature, living room, me and the world* and *dreams*. The rest of the materials flow in and out of a large depot, in response to the interests of the young customers and the keen team of children's librarians. The vibrant centre is the Atelier, the workshop, where children can process and design information and inspiration in any form they wish. This makes the library an Explorium, an inviting place to discover things, to dig deeply into a subject, to show findings and results and especially, to share those with other children.

Figure 10. Hard at work?

Inspiring

Many libraries in the Netherlands, but also in other countries, are interested in these developments and the concept has been presented at conferences and meetings in Denmark, Sweden, Ireland and Germany. The intention is to give children the feeling they can go anywhere they want and that there are many ways and possibilities to do this. The 'Library of 100 Talents' offers a framework for developing a truly new library, which is conscious of the children's needs in all of the services it offers. It is a matter of dialogue, reciprocity, exchange and dynamics through communicating with all senses, observing and discovering new angles, cooperating, amazement, growing, informing, getting started, showing and telling. The collection inspires and stimulates, but also irritates and intrigues. Programming is not always geared towards what is expected, but inspires new ideas, alternatives and routes other than the road well-trodden.

Figure 11. A library for all the senses

References

100x Glossy over de bibliotheek van 100 talenten [100x Magazine about the library of the 100 talents] (2011) Hoofddorp: Probiblio.

Bertrams, Karen and Mosch, Monique (2008) *"Je kan hier overal heen, bijna...": Samen bouwen aan een nieuwe jeugdbibliotheek* ["Here you can go everywhere you want, sort of...": Building an New Children's Library] Leidschendam: Uitgeverij Biblion. – ISBN 978-90-5483-818-0; PPN 312657323

Bruijnzeels, Rob and Tiggelen, Nicoline van (2001) *Bibliotheken 2040: De toekomst in uitvoering* [Libraries 2040: Execution of the future] Leischendam: Uitgeverij Biblion.

De bibliotheek van de 100 talenten [The library of the 100 talents] (2010) Leidschendam: Biblion Uitgeverij. Texts both available in Dutch and English. ISBN 978-90-5483-934-7. Includes:

1. Leenheers, Pam (2010) *Je kunt het!* [You can do it!] [ed. Rob Bruijnzeels, et al.] Leidschendam: Biblion Uitgeverij. (De bibliotheek van de 100 talenten / The library of the 100 talents). Texts both available in Dutch and English.

2. *Het idee* [The idea] (2010) [ed. Rob Bruijnzeels, et al.] Leidschendam: Biblion Uitgeverij. (De bibliotheek van de 100 talenten / The library of the 100 talents). Texts both available in Dutch and English.

3. *Het kan* [It can be done] (2010) [ed. Rob Bruijnzeels, et al.] Leidschendam: Biblion Uitgeverij. (De bibliotheek van de 100 talenten / The library of the 100 talents). Texts both available in Dutch and English.

Gardner, Howard (1993) *Multiple Intelligences: New Horizons*. New York: Basic Books.

More information:

Karen Bertrams, library consultant ProBiblio (provinces North & South Holland) , focus on children & innovation. Mail: kbertrams@probiblio.nl; Phone: 0031 (0) 6-24556381

Children's Spaces From Around The World

Kathleen R.T. Imhoff
Library consultant at Library Consulting Inc.;
Lexington, Kentucky, U.S.A.

Introduction

Integrating the three universal "A's" of good building design into the planning process is critical when designing library spaces for young children anywhere in the world. The three "A's" of building design are: adaptability, accessibility and aesthetics.

This article demonstrates the importance of these principles in designing innovative children's spaces and places in public libraries throughout the world. Discussed in this paper are the Amsterdam Public Library, The Netherlands, Lexington Public Library, Lexington, Kentucky, USA, Asker and the Oslo Public Libraries in Norway, the Minneapolis Public Library, Minneapolis, Minnesota, USA, Cerretos Public Library, California, USA, Durban Public Library, Durban, South Africa and the Indianapolis Public Library in Indianapolis, Indiana, USA.

As the world, particularly for children, continues rapidly to change pace, it is necessary to design adaptable, flexible, child-centred spaces to meet the informational, educational and recreational needs of children. In the past, many children's areas were well-defined rooms separated from the rest of the library area. In the hundreds of Carnegie libraries built in the early 1900's in England, Scotland and the United States, the children's department was usually located in the basement of the library building. It was often accessed by a steep stairway which was not safe for parents holding stacks of books or their children's hands, or for toddlers. Often these children's areas, although spacious, had inadequate lighting, small, high windows, were damp and being located in a basement, felt like a second class space. Many of the old Carnegie Libraries were retrofitted with better lighting and ramps for accessibility, but they still remained a basement space.

In libraries built in the 1960-90's, children's areas received more attention and often included separate, purpose-built rooms for story telling or for craft activities, with sinks, craft tables and storage space for craft materials. Many had amenities such as stroller parking areas, separate child-sized or family bathrooms, facilities for diaper changing and rocking chairs for parents and caregivers with young children to enjoy. Most of the children's spaces built during this period were large, open areas with closed door story rooms being replaced by corners with mats that could be used for other activities when not in use for story time.

Adaptability

With the ever increasing building costs and the pace of world change, it is difficult to foresee and plan what an ideal child centred space will be five years from now. However, adaptability and flexibility in children's space is increasingly important when planning a new library building or remodelling an older one.

Libraries in Europe introduced the adaptable concept of shelves on wheels to allow for maximum flexibility for all spaces. This concept works particularly well in children's space. Libraries in America did not begin to use shelves on wheels until a few years ago. Illustrations 1 and 2 show the central area in the Village Branch Library, in Lexington, Kentucky.

Village Branch, Lexington KY   Photography by Kathleen Imhoff

Figure 1. Shelving on wheels

Village Branch, Lexington KY   Photography by Kathleen Imhoff

Figure 2. Space created for performing

The first picture shows the library with the shelves in place to accommodate the children's collection of materials. With the shelves being on wheels, the staff can easily push them together or move them into another room to allow space for the showing of a popular children's program. The space created by moving the shelves allows for a larger audience than the library's meeting room would accommodate.

Another way of making a space adaptable is using sliding glass doors. These doors allow the same space to be used for two functions at different times of the day. It avoids special purpose rooms, such as story hour rooms, sitting vacant and unused when a particular activity is not scheduled. In addition, by using glass door walls, it allows people using the contiguous space to see the activity going on in the room. This design element acts as a marketing tool. This same concept, sliding glass doors, can be used effectively with children's computer space. The glass doors are closed when a class is in session, but opened at non-class times so all of the computers are accessible when a class is not being taught.

Northside Branch, Lexington, KY   Photography by Kathleen Imhoff

Figure 3. Story space

The picture of the Northside Branch Library of the Lexington Public Library shows the children's story space glassed and enclosed (Figure 3). The doors are open unless a story hour is being held or special children's activities are going on.

Amsterdam, Netherlands   Photography by Kathleen Imhoff

Figure 4. Shelving in children's area, Amsterdam Public Library

Multi-functional meeting spaces enhance the usability of children's areas. In visiting libraries in various parts of the world, I have observed children's meeting spaces being used for display space for children's art and craft projects, displays of local children's illustrators, for special collections of books for children and for children's programs.

Shelving that allows for multiple uses also works very well for children. Shelving designs for children's materials change. Some of these adaptations include wider shelves for easy books, hanging rods for cassettes and books packaged in large bags, narrow shelves to accommodate videos, and special shelving or bins for CDs, and DVDs. Many companies have specially designed low custom units for very young children as well as units that accommodate face-out shelving or shelving with many different types of formats in the same unit. Some libraries use low cost laundry baskets for easy storage of children's board books. Shelving should be of a height appropriate for the age group using the materials. Ideally shelving should not be over 42 inches (106.68 cm) and never over 60 inches (152.4 cm). Shelving or spaces for accessible storage for games, puzzles, board books, music and easy reading placed with front covers facing out, all need to be considered in planning for usable children's spaces.

Accessibility

Accessibility, the second "A" of good building design, is of particular importance in areas to be used by children. It is necessary to define the age of the children the space should serve. Since children grow at their own individual pace, the children's space should be easily accessible for all. Space which is easy to navigate with children in strollers, parking space for the strollers, designated but confined spaces for children who crawl, are all examples of accessibility.

Furniture needs to be considered when designing for accessibility in a children's area. After the age of the users has been defined, size-appropriate furniture should be included in a children's area. The error of purchasing too much furniture for very young children should be avoided. Small children often prefer to sit on the floor and like the challenge of sitting on a bigger chair. However, it is next to impossible for an adult or older child to sit on the very small furniture found in some children's departments.

All of the service desks and children's tables need to be wheelchair accessible and easily approachable for children. Look for service desks that can be easily height adjustable for staff on different shifts. Devices such as low vision machines, computers with adaptive features and children's Braille books might require special, larger spaces or furniture. Know your community and plan for the special needs that children in your area might have. Then, translate these needs into your building space planning and furniture selection.

Aesthetics

The third "A" of good building design is aesthetics. Aesthetic considerations are paramount when planning spaces for children. This element makes the difference as to whether or not a library space will serve as a magnet for children and as a place in which they want to spend their time; conversely if the aesthetic is not good then the library space can become a place in which they are not comfortable.

Decorative and innovative treatments to the entrances of a children's area automatically attract children and invite them to explore the space. Many libraries choose to spend a large part of their special feature and design budget on the entrance to the children's room. Libraries have created entrances that make children think they are entering a cave, an adventure area, or an open book. The Jacksonville Public Library in Jacksonville, Florida, U.S.A. adopted a wetlands theme, consistent with their local environment, for the entrance to the children's area. The entrance is a passageway of head-high sculpted grasses complete with the sounds of cricket, cicadas and tree frogs. Another feature of their entrance is a talking owl.

Cerretos, California   Photography by Kathleen Imhoff

Figure 5. Entrance with a difference

Other libraries have special features inside the library for children to provide them with a child-sized place of their own. The Richmond Public Library in British Columbia, Canada has a children's small-scale house with cosy seating and inviting books inside it to attract children to their special space. The Asker Public Library in Norway has a climbing wall for adventurous climbers in the children's area.

Many libraries have murals painted by local artists, famous illustrators of children's books or by the children themselves. These murals serve as magnets to draw children into the space. The Richland County Public Library in Columbia, South Carolina, USA has colourful, twelve foot cut-outs of Max and the Wild Things from the Maurice Sendak book, *Where the Wild Things Are,* as the signature entrance to their children's room. The Amsterdam Public Library in the Netherlands has adventure and learning areas defined by curved, sculpted shelving which accommodates media, books and computers as well as display space arranged by topics such as wonder, travel and imagination. The imagination space has a curved stairway up to a tower space on top of the shelving.

Olso, Norway   Photography by Kathleen Imhoff

Figure 6. Mural

Aesthetically pleasing signage which provides easy wayfinding for children, their parents and caregivers can also serve as a design element. Some libraries have abandoned typical library language such as circulation or reference and have substituted child-friendly, easy-to-understand words such as "Help" or "Info". Creative use of lettering in the signage can also make the signs design elements as well.

Cerretos, CA   Photography by Kathleen Imhoff

Figure 7. Signage, Cerretos

The use of strong colours can be a low-cost way of defining children's spaces. In a very small library on an economy budget, painting the children's area a bright, new colour is a way of improving the aesthetics. Painting large wooden cubes or crates in different primary colours for book shelving or storage, a night sky painted on the ceiling, and a child-sized entrance door are inexpensive ways of introducing colour into a children's area. Wooden shelving can be painted a bright colour to change the look of a space. Paint is one of the cheapest design elements. Work with the design team and your staff to think of creative ways to use colour.

Themed graphics appropriate to the local area is another way to attract children. Children are attracted to interactive spaces with attractive features. A large scale friendly animal, a tree with a smiling, welcoming cat or bird in its branches, a Thomas the Tank Engine play table, a climbing space, a boat, a night sky, a child-sized door or themed book cases are a few feature items that have been used successfully in public library children's spaces.

Many libraries have used puppet theatres as special interest items. Theatres can be built into a multi-use space or be portable and brought out when needed. Several libraries have used displays of puppets as a design feature.

Increasingly, libraries are including outside spaces for children in their designs. Butterfly or flower gardens as well as outside sculpture gardens are found in many new libraries. Outdoor areas that can be accessed directly from the children's department can be used for story times or programs when the weather permits.

Conclusion

Northside Library, Lexington, KY   Photography by Kathleen Imhoff

Figure 8. Themed book display units, Lexington

Think of the unique feature of your town, city or country and decide if that feature could be integrated into the children's library area in an appealing way. If you have a local children's illustrator, see if you can get permission to enlarge his or her pictures on a children's wall as a feature. The possibilities of unique special features that can be successfully used in a space for children are almost limitless and imagination can know no bounds The feature you use to make your children's space special is the unique feature that will keep kids coming back time after time.

For inspiration, visit other children's spaces: children's museums, innovative schools, children's theatres, children's bookstores, children's gardens and children's parks. Seek out pictures of children's libraries featured in architectural issues of library journals. Pick a few metropolitan cities from your country and also other parts of the world and take a virtual web tour to look at their children's areas. Look for the places where children are to be found and try to determine what attracted them to that space. Talk with children about their likes and dislikes.

Minneapolis Public Library, MN   Photography by Kathleen Imhoff

Figure 9. IT holds not fears

Remember the three architectural "A's": adaptability, accessibility and aesthetics. Learn from other successful children's libraries and spaces and have fun designing the best public library for the young children in your part of the world.

Conclusion

The collaboration between the IFLA Section for Library Buildings and Equipment (http://www.ifla.org/en/library-buildings-and-equipment) and the IFLA Section for Libraries for Children and Young Adults (http://www.ifla.org/en/libraries-for-children-and-ya) proved to be an extremely fruitful one with each group learning a great deal from the other. The design of libraries is undergoing much change in the 21st century as technology increasingly impacts on both the way we use libraries and the way we design them. The move from collection-centric spaces to user-centric ones has been well-documented and in designing spaces for children in libraries it is particularly important to recognize the needs of the people who use them. As can be seen from the contributions to this publication many imaginative solutions have resulted from the careful balancing of frivolity and functionality.

Information and design professionals who are involved in new library or refurbishment projects have to understand the needs of their users and of the communities in which the library plays, or should play, a central role. The library has, of course, to be fit for purpose but it also needs to be a welcoming, accessible and enjoyable place to be. Children need spaces that spark the imagination and give them the freedom to play, learn, express themselves and have fun. This gives the architect and library planner plenty of scope to give free rein to their imagination and allows them, too, to be more playful in their approach than is possible perhaps when designing other library building types.

The papers presented at the IFLA Milan conference and published here clearly illustrate common themes in children's libraries around the world. These include the use of colour and of artwork and graphics to provide stimulation, funky furniture, a variety of spaces both secret and open, performance space of some kind such as puppet and traditional theatres and areas for drawings and other achievements to be displayed. Places with special themes was another notable trend with Jacksonville Public Library in Florida leading the way with its interior design reflecting its environmental context – the under 12 area resembling the swamplands of north-east Florida and the teen area more "clubhouse cool" picking up the theme of the nearby ocean with wave-like ceiling features. All papers stressed the importance of getting children actively involved in the library and indeed in the design and furnishing of the building itself.

This publication serves two functions. Firstly, it provides an accurate and valuable description of the development and current state of the design of children's libraries around the world with many exciting and inspiring examples of recent projects. Secondly, it points the way to the future by looking at recent trends – technological and social – that affect the way we approach the design of children's libraries. The case studies included here also provide ideas for how we can incrementally change and improve library spaces to move with the times even if money is not available for large-scale projects. It is clear that if we are to provide libraries designed for the children of the 21st century then we need to take account of changing ways of learning and integrate new technology with traditional materials. We need to embrace the future while not losing the best of the old. Only then can we ensure that the library remains at the centre of its community and important in children's lives.

Ingrid Bon
and
Karen Latimer

Author Biographies

ALISTAR BLACK has been a full Professor in the Graduate School of Library and Information Science, University of Illinois at Urbana-Champaign, USA since January 2009, having previously taught and researched for 19 years at Leeds Metropolitan University, UK. He is author of the following books: *A New History of the English Public Library* (1996) and *The Public Library in Britain 1914-2000* (2000). He is also co-author of *Understanding Community Librarianship* (1997); *The Early Information Society in Britain, 1900-1960* (2007); and *Books, Buildings and Social Engineering* (2009), a socio-architectural history of early public libraries in Britain. With Peter Hoare, he edited Volume 3 (covering 1850-2000) of the *Cambridge History of Libraries in Britain and Ireland* (2006). He was Chair of the Library History Group of the Library Association, 1992-9; and of the IFLA Section on Library History, 2003-7. He was editor of the international journal *Library History*, 2004-8; and is currently North American editor of *Library and Information History*. He is co-editor of the journal *Library Trends*. He has recently been researching the history of corporate libraries and staff magazines, and the design of public libraries in the 1960s.

CAROLYNN RANKIN is a senior lecturer in the School of Applied Global Ethics, Faculty of Health and Social Sciences at Leeds Metropolitan University in the UK. Carolynn lectures on masters and undergraduate courses on the information society, global citizenship and research methods. She worked for 20 years in special and academic library and information services as an information specialist and library manager before moving into professional education in 2000. Carolynn is a Member of the Chartered Institute of Library and Information Professionals (CILIP) and External Examiner for the CILIP Chartership Board. Her current research interests include the social impact of information and library services and the role of the information professional.

Carolynn has been invited to lecture to professional associations and conferences in Europe and Canada. She has directed research projects including the *National Year of Reading* evaluation in Yorkshire and is undertaking research on the 'Sister Libraries Programme' of the Libraries for Children and Young Adults Section of IFLA. She was the lead author for *'Delivering the Best Start: a Guide to Early Years Libraries'* published by Facet and is editing a follow up book focusing on the challenges of delivering library services to children and young adults in the digital age.

KIRSTEN DROTNER is a professor in the Department of Literature, Culture and Media Studies at the University of Southern Denmark and founding director of DREAM: Danish Research Centre on Education and Advanced Media Materials. Author or editor of 15 books and more than 100 articles and book chapters, her research interests include media history, qualitative methodologies, and young people's media uses. Her most recent work focuses on social media and creative content creation as developed in out-of-school contexts such as museums and libraries. Her latest publication is *Digital Content Creation: Perceptions, Practices and Perspectives* (Peter Lang 2010, co-editor Kim Christian Schrøder).

JAMES R. KELLER, AIA, is a partner with the multi-disciplined architectural/engineering firm VITETTA, based in Philadelphia. Mr. Keller created the VITETTA Library Design Studio in 1996. Since then, he has provided the design vision and project direction for several significant American Library systems including the Free Library of Philadelphia, San Antonio Public Library, TX, Broward County Public Library, FL and Lexington Public Library, KY. Mr. Keller has also designed Libraries in South America and the Middle East and has forged international Library design collaborations with Schmidt Hammer Lassen of Denmark and Foster and Partners of London.

Recent projects include the new Children's Public Library in Muscat, Oman – to be the first public Library in Oman – unique in its design and service model in the Middle East. Mr. Keller provided design leadership and guidance in the creation of the largest public Library ever constructed in Chile. At over 200,000 square feet of space, this Library is an overwhelming success – a true destination for Chileans and international visitors.

Mr. Keller has developed an internationally respected expertise in library design and is completing a soon to be published book on designing space for children with co-author Sandra Feinberg, MLS, for ALA Publications. Mr. Keller promotes functional design that supports the mission of library service and embraces architectural and interior design excellence. Mr. Keller believes that the evolving mission and nature of library service must be accommodated by flexible, creative design that renders itself through lasting architectural presence.

DR H. INCI ÖNAL is an Associate Professor at the Department of Information Management at Hacettepe University in Ankara, Turkey. Her research focus is on school librarianship, media studies, information resources, genealogy, local history, archives, children's literature and the information-seeking behaviour of children and young adults. She holds graduate degrees in Library and Information Studies (MA and PhD) from the University of Hacettepe. Dr Önal has lectured on school librarianship courses arranged by the Ministry of National Education. She completed nationwide studies and projects about students', journalists' and historians' information requirements, improving the existing situation and the new information technologies. She was a member of the IFLA Standing Committee on School Libraries and Resource Centres and also contributed to the preparation of the IFLA / UNESCO School Library Manifesto. In 2004 she received the Takeshi Murofushi Research Award given by International Association of School Librarianship (IASL) for her project on 'School libraries of one world: the influence of standards'. Her recent research publications include "New developments on the Turkish school library scene", *Journal of Librarianship and Information Science 2005,* 37 (3): 141-152; and "IFLA / UNESCO School Library Manifesto for creating one world: Germany, Iran and Turkey in comparative perspective". *Libri* 2009, 59 (1): 45-54. She may be contacted by e-mail at onal@hacettepe.edu.tr.

ALEXANDER LAMIS, AIA, is a Partner at Robert A.M. Stern Architects and is a member of its management committee. An authority on library design, Mr. Lamis has designed public libraries in Jacksonville, Miami Beach, and Clearwater, Florida; Nashville, Tennessee; Columbus, Georgia; Southport, Connecticut; Bangor, Maine; Lakewood, Ohio; Calabasas, California; New York; and Chapel Hill, North Carolina; as well as the Baker Library | Bloomberg Center at the Harvard Business School. He is currently working on the George W. Bush Presidential Library at Southern Methodist University in Dallas.

A frequent speaker on library issues, Mr. Lamis has made presentations at *Computers in Libraries, IOLS,* the National Library of Medicine, the PLA National Conference, and the 2009 IFLA Annual Conference in Milan. An active member of LLAMA, he has served on the Program Committee, the Architecture for Public Libraries Committee, and the College and University Buildings Committee. He was program chair and speaker for *Going Green Without Going Broke,* a discussion of sustainable design solutions in libraries for the 2002 ALA national convention, which was repeated at the 2004 Convention. He contributed a chapter on sustainable design in libraries to the book *Planning the Modern Public Library Building* (Westport, Connecticut: Libraries Unlimited, 2003) and the article "Evolving Spaces: An Architect's Perspective on Libraries" to Volume 28 of *Advances in Librarianship* (Oxford, England: Elsevier, 2004).

Mr. Lamis holds a Bachelor of Science degree from the Massachusetts Institute of Technology and a Master of Architecture degree from the Graduate School of Architecture and Planning of Columbia University, where he was a Kinne Fellow and was awarded the AIA Certificate of Merit. Mr. Lamis is a member of the American Institute of Architects, and the American Library Association, and is a registered architect in eleven states.

BARBARA A.B. GUBBIN. As the Library Director of the Jacksonville Public Library in Jacksonville, Florida (USA), Barbara Gubbin oversees a large urban public library system with a Main Library and 20 branch libraries. Ms. Gubbin directed the final implementation of the library's Better Jacksonville Plan projects in 2005, opening four of six new branches and a new Main Library. At the completion of the library construction projects, Ms. Gubbin guided the library's community planning process, resulting in Destination: next, Jacksonville Public Library's five year strategic plan.

Ms. Gubbin began her career as a young adult librarian at the San Antonio Public Library in San Antonio, Texas. Ms. Gubbin joined the Houston Public Library, becoming its director in 1995. As Library Director of the Houston Public Library, Ms. Gubbin was responsible for a Central Library and 39 other library facilities and oversaw both new library construction and extensive renovation projects. She was also responsible for the implementation of a new integrated library system and brought web-based services through the library to the Houston community.

Ms. Gubbin holds a Masters of Library and Information Studies from the University of London, University College. Ms. Gubbin's professional activities include serving as Secretary to the International Federation of Library Association's Committee for Public Libraries. She serves on the Board of the Florida Library Association and North East Florida Library Information Network. Ms. Gubbin is a Past President of the Texas Library Association (1996); served on the OCLC Board of Trustees for six years (1999-2004) and recently co-chaired the OCLC Records Use Policy Council.

Since the opening of the new libraries in Jacksonville all library activity indicators have climbed: circulation of library materials by 49% and the number of visitors by 39%. In 2009 Jacksonville Public Library circulated 9.1M items, saw 5.4M visitors and 5.1M hits to its website.

GONZALO OYARZÚN is currently the National Coordinator of the Public Libraries System of Chile, a member of Libraries, Archives and Museums Directorate of Chile (DIBAM) – an institution leads and manages the entire system of public libraries in Chile.

He was a founding director of the Santiago Public Library. From the beginning of this Project, he has played an integral role in its formation, design, implementation and habilitation.

Prior to that, he has developed professionally in different areas of library science in Chile, involving the academic scope, public and private companies, libraries and specialized documents centers. He has participated in the creation, administration and direction of innovative projects and programs, including national planning on new technologies. He has written in publications about public libraries and is an advocate of reading.

Also, he has been a member of the International Federation of Library Associations (IFLA), in the Public Libraries and Latin America and the Caribbean Sections. Gonzalo was born in Santiago de Chile and studied Literature.

TONE LUNDEN works at Hjørring Libraries as a children's librarian and as a children's library consultant. She has worked on a number of development projects such as the"The children's library as experimentarium", the Nordic project "The Northern Word" and the Dutch Nordic project "Making Tracks". Tone was a member of the steering group for the new main library in Hjørring which opened in April 2008.

KAREN BERTRAMS – Arnhem, Netherlands, 1960.
Started in 1982 as a children's librarian in Amsterdam public library (OBA). Since 1991 working for provincial library organization ProBiblio on topics like; library innovation – participation and co-creation of user groups in libraries – mixed media use in programming for libraries – international lectures and presentations about libraries in relation to media and users – development of the Library of 100 Talents; multiple intelligent libraries / Reggio – networking with art & science scenes.

Contact information: Karen Bertrams, library advisor ProBiblio. MOB 0031(0)6-24556381 . MAIL kbertrams@probiblio.nl.

MONIQUE MOSCH – Alkmaar, Netherlands, 1962.
After the Library Academy she has been working in public libraries for children. During that time she developed several educational programs on children's literature and bookpromotion.

In the public library of Heerhugowaard she developed (together with children, architects, designers and librarians) a very special children's department based on pedagogical ideas like multiple intelligence, children participation and the theory of Loris Malaguzzi : the library of 100 talents. She is now working as advisor for libraries, bookstores and pedagogical institutions.

Contact information: mail mam.mosch@quicknet.nl or mob 0031(0)6-53193549

KATHLEEN R.T. IMHOFF is a Library Consultant with years of experience in the public library field. An M.L.S. graduate of the University of Wisconsin-Madison, U.S.A. she is a well-known lecturer, writer, workshop leader, technology innovator and change agent.

Having worked as a Director in small, rural libraries, a medium-sized library, a state library Agency and major urban libraries, she bring a unique perspective to creating library spaces for the children of today and tomorrow. She has travelled extensively in many counties visiting premier, innovative children's libraries. She has incorporated the most successful of these ideas into the children's libraries she designs. At Broward County Library, Ft. Lauderdale, Florida, the ninth largest library in the United State, she was the Children's Coordinator and designed over twenty children's spaces in new branch and regional libraries. The Broward County Library was named the 1996-97 "Library Journal/Gale, Library of the Year".

An active member of state, regional, national and international library associations, she served two terms as Councilor of the American Library Association, President of the Public Relations Section, twice President of the Public Library System Section of the Public Library Association. She is currently the President of the South-eastern Library Association, a member of the American Library Association's Building Award Committee and a member of the Metropolitan Library Section of the International Federation of Library Associations.

She is part of the design term for the first public library in Muscat, Oman. The library will be an innovative, five story all children's library located on the Gulf of Oman.